Louis van Gaal Coaching Philosophy and Practices

MW00818063

Published by

SOCCER TUTOR
.COM

Louis van Gaal's

Coaching Philosophy and Practices

First Published October 2014 by SoccerTutor.com

Info@soccertutor.com | www.SoccerTutor.com

UK: 0208 1234 007 | US: (305) 767 4443 | **ROTW:** +44 208 1234 007

ISBN 978-1-910491-01-0

Original Dutch Publishers

DeVoetbalTrainer ©, All Rights Reserved - www.devoetbaltrainer.nl

Edited by

Alex Fitzgerald - SoccerTutor.com

Cover & Book Design by

Alex Macrides, Think Out Of The Box Ltd.
email: design@thinkootb.com Tel: +44 (0) 208 144 3550

Pictures by

Pro Shots - www.proshots.nl

Diagrams

Diagram designs by SoccerTutor.com. All the diagrams in this book have been created using SoccerTutor.com Tactics Manager Software available from
www.SoccerTutor.com

Note: While every effort has been made to ensure the technical accuracy of the content of this book, neither the author nor publishers can accept any responsibility for any injury or loss sustained as a result of the use of this material

CONTENTS

CHAPTER 1

CHAPTER 2

CHAPTER 3

CHAPTER 4

CONTENTS

CHAPTER 5

CHAPTER 6

CONTENTS

CHAPTER 1

Pre-World Cup 2014 Analysis: The 3-5-2 / 3-4-1-2 Formation

A First Analysis of Netherlands' New Style of Play: The 3-5-2 / 3-4-1-2

WC 2014: After Netherlands vs Ecuador (Pre-World Cup Warm Up Game)

On May 12th 2014, Netherlands played in a new formation. It was invariably called the 5-3-2 system by the media, but in practice it's quite difficult to provide a single name for it. Is it 5-3-2, 3-5-2, 3-4-3 or 3-4-1-2? The name actually isn't that important. The system depends on the opposition's style of play, the location of the ball and the exact situation during the match. Which team has the ball and where on the pitch? Logically the most important thing is the concept of play within, and the practical implementation of the style of play by the players. Here we have an analysis of this game.

After the match, Netherlands head coach Louis van Gaal called the style of play 3-4-3. He thereby counted Wijnaldum as a 'number 10' with the forwards, and the wing backs were counted as midfielders. In our analysis of Netherlands vs Ecuador, we choose to call it the 3-4-1-2 formation, but we do realise the relativity of it.

The entire editorial staff of De Voetbaltrainer was invited by Eisma Business Media to attend the Netherlands vs Ecuador match. We asked a well respected employee of De Voetbaltrainer, Rob Baan, for his insights in response to this match.

Rob Baan: "In the Netherlands, the discussion about the concept of play Louis van Gaal will use in the World Cup after the friendly match Netherlands vs Ecuador has rather increased - then decreased. However, a few comments can be made.

First of all, I'm convinced that every World Cup country pretty much adapts its system to the strengths and weaknesses of the opposition. The Netherlands will play differently against Australia than they will against Spain or Chile. In this warm up phase of preparation, the coach especially wants to test which players are able to function within a system that could possibly be the starting point in certain World Cup matches. With a number of players you think you already know, and with other players you might still be hesitant. The friendly games are successful if those doubts have been allayed."

WHAT DID LOUIS VAN GAAL LEARN FROM NETHERLANDS VS ECUADOR?

Rob Baan: "In the backline, Veltman and Kongolo do not (yet) meet the criteria for the way in which Van Gaal wants the 3-4-1-2 concept put into action. Within that concept there is a crucial role for the wing-backs. They need to find the right moment on the sides, have the guts and technical skills to pass an opponent, and be able to deliver a good cross.

But in that position it's also mainly a matter of making the right decisions; when do you decide to go for it, when do you press high up the pitch, when do you go for the combination, and when do you have to enter a 1v1 against an opponent? But mainly also; When are you not allowed to go, and do you carry out your basic tasks as a defender in a good way? At this time, of the available wing backs, only Janmaat has the desired level when it comes to making the right decision, in relation to a good execution. Van Aanholt performed a lot better than Kongolo in the second half, but Van Gaal will have to discuss certain choices with him. Another important requirement for the defenders within this concept is the mutual collaboration. Although, relatively very few chances were given away, the collaboration definitely wasn't ideal yet. The goal conceded was an excellent and useful example for this, but certainly not the only one."

The Netherlands 3-4-1-2 Formation vs Ecuador

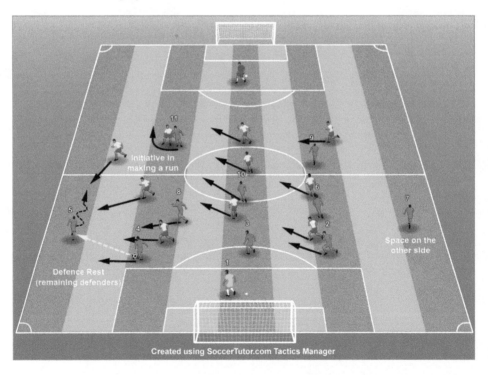

BUILD UP PLAY

Rob Baan: "The build-up play from the back is crucial in this concept. If the build-up is too slow and no one has the guts to push forward, then you make it very easy for the opposition. They can effortlessly move along and wait until the Netherlands lose possession. This week, in Portugal, they will undoubtedly train more often on playing the ball forward quicker and daring to push forward into the centre from the back with the ball.

SET COMBINATION PLAY

In the upcoming training sessions they will certainly also focus a lot on set combinations/movements. The goal from the Netherlands of course was of great class, and the pass from Clasie to Van Persie was of world class level. This specific quality of the Feyenoord midfielder to unexpectedly set up someone free in front of the goalkeeper becomes an increasingly dangerous weapon if there is more set combination play. Meanwhile, in the so often quoted interview by Van Gaal in De Voetbaltrainer, he also announced that he plans to spend a lot of energy during preparation on switching play with long balls, because the space is always on the other side. The execution of the cross pass against Ecuador was quite moderate. Over the ground it looked good at times, especially from left to right, but through the air the execution was definitely not good enough. This requires more training time and practice.

CONCLUSION

Van Gaal has certainly become wiser after this game. He has especially gained more insight into the question: Who is not ready to carry out the desired 3-4-1-2 formation, and what deserves extra attention in the coming weeks? It wouldn't surprise me at all if he tested the 3-4-1-2 formation again during the next friendly against Ghana. By doing this he'll gain insight into the functioning of the players within this concept, who will join this week, but he'll also most likely make different tactical choices in the last friendly game against Wales."

CHAPTER

2

Preparation and Tactics for the 2014 World Cup

Text: Paul Geerars and Tjeu Seeverens

Preparation and Tactics for the 2014 World Cup

'I Prefer to Select Players with Sufficient Vision and Awareness'

It's autumn 2001. Rinus Michels has expressed his preference for a hotel in the immediate vicinity of his apartment in Amsterdam-Zuid. There the interview will take place for the cover article of the first anniversary edition of this magazine, VT 100. Therefore, because it has to be something special, on the intercession of "the General" the then Netherlands coach Louis van Gaal has also been invited. What we knew gets confirmed that afternoon; both top coaches have a tremendous amount of respect for each other. The picture of the two, a physically weak looking Rinus Michels sitting in a leather armchair with Louis van Gaal rising high above him as a commander, is the most beautiful in the history of De Voetbaltrainer.

At that moment Van Gaal didn't know yet that he would experience the biggest disappointment in his career a few weeks later, as the unexpected loss against Ireland blocked the participation of the Netherlands in the 2002 World Cup in Japan and South Korea.

March 2014. The same Louis van Gaal will this time go to the World Cup with the Netherlands after an impressive qualifying campaign. At the start of the mission in September 2012, he explained to this magazine already (exclusively) how he will be working with his staff until the last match of the Dutch national team in Brazil. Yet as a specialist he appears to be prepared to share sufficient information just before the preparation with his fellow coaches once again.

NO TRENDS

Will the World Cup in Brazil be a tournament where we will see any new trends in top football?

Louis van Gaal: "There are hardly any new developments when it comes to the style of play, and I don't expect this to happen during this World Cup.

The wheel has already been invented a long time ago. As of 2014, head coaches of a national team let their teams play in a 4-4-2 or 4-3-3 formation. Almost all decisions are derived from there. Only very few times will a colleague opt for another system, because the culture lends itself for it. For instance, Cesare Prandelli of Italy started with a five-man defence in the heavily charged opening match versus Spain during the previous European Championship. It ended in a draw, but the Italians should have won that game. Yet Prandelli, a very modern coach, also rapidly switched over to a 4-4-2 formation afterwards. I found that strange, but in consultation with his players he returned back to the familiar system.

During my whole career I've been choosing the 4-3-3 system as a foundation. For the Dutch national team so far (prior to Ecuador match and the 2014 World Cup) I have only exchanged the game concept in the midfield. As a club coach I've sometimes made other decisions, by altering the defensive structure with, for instance, three instead of four defenders if the opposition played with two strikers. You can't just do this without thinking, it requires a lot of work during training and you don't generally have that time as a coach of a national team. You do as a manager of a club however, but even at Ajax in the same way, the option of playing with three defenders against two strikers

has vanished from the club culture. Under Frank de Boer, Ajax basically always plays with four players in the back. The full backs do however push forward a lot when Ajax have possession, but the defensive midfielder pushes backwards during the first phase of ball possession to create a 3v2 situation. That's why Ajax still plays with 1 deep lying midfielder. It is only when Ajax come to play in the third or fourth phase of ball possession, then the player occupies the position again in the midfield. You keep seeing this more and more in international football. In that respect Frank de Boer has been quite a trendsetter, yes. What I notice, is that at many teams, the defensive midfielder, the number 6, moves backwards too soon. If the opposition doesn't apply immediate pressure, then you unnecessarily have a player too deep and separate from the rest of the midfield. My perspective here differs.

If the selected players are accustomed to playing with four defenders, then we would not normally play with three defenders at a World Cup. That's why, from day one, I've expressed my preference for four defenders and a midfield with 1 deep/defensive midfielder. Sometimes we've adjusted this during the game by playing with two defensive midfielders, because Van der Vaart and Sneijder to date do not function sufficiently in a midfield with only one defensive midfielder. The players have to be at top fitness for this, both physically and mentally. So these two will only have a few months remaining for this, because at the World Cup, if I have all players at my disposal, my preference will be for a midfield positioning with one defensive midfielder. This is also because most South American teams don't play with two strikers."

8

'Most progress has been made during ball possession for when the opposition have good defensive organisation.'

COACHING LANGUAGE

The coaches of the national youth teams don't speak about 1 or 2 defensive midfielders, but about a dynamic midfield...

Louis van Gaal: "That's the discussion I'm currently having with the KNVB. I like practice and I speak the language that corresponds to it. Around me I mainly hear technical terms during coaching, even sentences from the action theory. In practice this works differently. When trying to teach, to me it seems better to continue identifying the four key moments and then divide them into stages. This makes it easier to understand for the players. By naming them, you can make the different stages of the key moments from the match trainable, and allow players to perform it in a better way."

TECHNICAL DIRECTOR

If you were still the coach after the World Cup, would you have engaged into the discussion more aggressively?

Louis van Gaal: "I've already been through that battle during my first term as coach of the Dutch national team. Back then I had a dual function; I was also a Technical Director. For a minute it looked like my vision would be widely supported within the KNVB. The language of coaching, the 'Master Plan' and my proposal about making the competition attractive for the first team, the second team; It was all accepted. But after I was gone for merely two months everything was called into question and inadequately carried out afterwards. This has everything to do with only one thing; within the KNVB they lack a Technical Director with esteem. Somebody

who checks the context every time and evaluates if everything agreed about the football development is actually being carried out the way it should over a period of 10 to 15 years.

After all these years it still appears to be a utopia that, besides Bert van Oostveen, Director of Professional Football KNVB, there will be a Technical Director with all the powers for both Professional Football and Amateur Football. There now is a Technical Manager, but he has neither power nor a budget. Then you can forget about any progress being made. Who would be a suitable candidate? Van Gaal in any case will go into retreat, and because of the necessary continuity it also shouldn't be any one of my age. Mohammed Allach, who has been Technical Manager for a bit, would have definitely been capable of it. He's a top professional, with whom I've had a great working relationship. But he also didn't have the budget, nor power and is therefore currently at Vitesse. Jesse Goes would be suitable. If you give someone like him the influence and the tools, then the esteem and power to really change things will come eventually by itself. He would also definitely need to gather the right people around him, because such a huge job, you can't do alone."

PROGRESS IN BUILD UP PLAY

Back to the topic of the Netherlands. On which tactical component has the team made most progress?

Louis van Gaal: "Most progress has been made during ball possession when the opposition has a good defensive organisation. When I started with this job it was looking very bad, especially the positional play during the first phase of the build-up play. That's not really surprising,

considering the fact that the Dutch squad mainly consists of players who hardly ever get in a situation to build up from the back at their clubs abroad. Thus they don't train this aspect either. Therefore, every week they play in a way that goes against the principles of the Dutch football philosophy. Even at the top clubs in England, nobody really cares if the goalkeeper just kicks the ball forward again and again. When we scout in the English competition for the Dutch national team, we always have to make that judgment whether the development of such a player still sufficiently matches our vision. But we're also making verifiable progress on this area with the Dutch national team. Meanwhile, in the past few matches of the qualification series and friendlies, we've still managed to score a decent number of goals during stages, wherein we could impose our will on our opponent by having good positional play. That's the main point. There aren't many countries that are capable of doing this. However, we still have to make progress in the coming months on this component, because the upcoming world champion will be the one who controls this the best."

BEING COMPACT IN DEFENCE

Louis van Gaal: "Another area where we've made significant steps is playing compact when the opposition has ball possession. The players know: the distance between the defensive line and the strikers has to be left as small as possible. During our first match versus Belgium it was still 30 metres.

Now we manage to not let that distance exceed more than 20 -25 metres during a large part of the match. Also of importance is the mutual distance of the defenders. This may never exceed 15 metres and we strive

for 5-10 metres depending on the game situation. The full backs have to be capable to read the shirt number of a central defender. At every back pass of the opposition we push forward. The central defenders watch out if no one keeps sticking around. If we win the ball, then depth goes above width, because the opposition usually isn't well organised then. During our games we've also managed to give away very few chances. This has a direct relation with playing as compact as possible when the opposition have possession and with the condition that no single player withdraws himself from that process.

A team has a defensive organisation, and at the Dutch national team the number 9's contribution is just as important as the number 1's contribution. They all participate. That's why we've hardly conceded any goals, not even when we played with 10 players for a long period against a top team like Colombia. That's something to be proud of. We're still making progress on that subject. This also applies to set pieces. Our opponents only profited from two penalties and we ourselves scored more than 10 times from set pieces, largely thanks to the superb technique of Sneijder and especially Van der Vaart."

PLAYER AWARENESS

Louis van Gaal: "Positioning compact' and 'remaining compact' are two terms which I did take from the KNVB, because these are easy to use terms that players understand right away. This also goes for 'positioning wide' during ball possession. This doesn't necessarily mean that you need to have chalk on your boots though, just like Robben says. If the ball goes through the lines dynamically during ball possession, then you mainly have to use your sense of awareness. This should ensure that 'standing

wide' means that you see which direction you have to follow to give your teammates the desired space to act quickly and effectively. With that sense of awareness you harmonise with each other quickly where you have to move. This is an important condition in top level football.

'Players with a poor sense of awareness are not ripe for the true top level, and I prefer to not select them.'

If I go to scout a potential new player for the Netherlands, I specifically pay attention to their sense of awareness, in addition to their physical fitness, mental fitness and passing within the profile for a specific position. Awareness is not only dependent on the ball and your teammates' positions, but always also the opposition. You can never do something on the pitch without taking into account the opposition. Therefore, in a training session at this level, exercises without resistance are less effective, including on the day prior to a match, even though someone could get injured by using that resistance.

To test the sense of awareness of new players within the Dutch squad, and to improve this in all players, I often choose the 5v3 possession exercise. This is the best drill to assess whether a player has that sense of awareness.

And also whether he has the technique to adjust the passing speed to the situation, in a small space under pressure with lots of triangles. It contains so much; you can prove with it that you will also survive in very small spaces by finding the free player. At the same time you also have to be capable of thinking strategically by luring an opponent in, before suddenly switching play with a pass at the right time. This isn't easy, trust me. Many players feel suffocated at first when they join the national team.

'To test the sense of awareness of new players within the Netherlands selection, and to improve this in all players, I often choose the 5v3 possession exercise.'

What's decisive for staying or dropping out: Do we see the player experiencing sufficient progress?

If you often play 5v3, you become better in it and you'll see it displayed during the matches."

In the last two years, we saw the Netherlands national team train in Katwijk, Kumarakom, various stadiums, during their training camp in Lagos (Portugal) and in Brazil during the World Cup.

The 5v3 possession exercise, according to Louis van Gaal, is well suited to judging the awareness of time and space. He used this exercise in the month building up to the World Cup to measure the potential of the players' awareness and positional play. Even during the World Cup, we saw this training exercise yet again.

Please see 5 v 3 AWARENESS AND POSSESSION EXERCISE **on Page 53**

Louis van Gaal: "Another drill we often choose is attack vs defence. For instance, we may train to tactically prepare the players for an opponent that is very defensive. We call it Plan B. We mainly coach the forwards on the solutions to disorganise such a defence.

Please see 6 v 7 (+GK) ATTACK VS DEFENCE PRACTICE **on Page 54**

As a club coach I often preferred to use 8v7 practices with one big goal without a goalkeeper. You then have to feel when the time is right to apply pressure as a collective or instead defend the empty goal. This is a drill I loved to give as a club coach."

Please see COLLECTIVE DEFENDING 8 v 7 GAME SITUATION **on Page 55**

THE OPPOSITION

Louis van Gaal: "There is always a relation with the specific qualities of the opposition and with how we stand compactly. For instance, during a World Cup it's very likely that there is an excellent opposition playmaker positioned in the midfield. This could mean that our defensive midfielder, the number 6, could give less backing to his teammates because he has to play closer to that playmaker. This has immediate consequences for how the central defenders should position themselves to combat the midfielders of the opposition who are pushing up. It's my and the staff's job to recognise this every time, and prepare our players properly for this. We do this over and over. So therefore, there is no such thing as one model about the desired execution of playing compact. We can however name some basic principles: the goal should be to stand as closely as possible to each other as a team, both vertically and horizontally, so you can always provide cover and deal with your own man.

In an ideal situation this means that in our vision the defensive line is positioned around halfway into your own half, so the space behind, during a cross field pass, can also be guarded and reached by a goalkeeper. The execution of this was really brilliant versus Colombia. Always on the edge, though. This was mainly because, and there you have it again, the specific qualities of a top team like Colombia. If you play as compact as the Netherlands, then

'There is no such thing as one model about the desired execution of playing compact. You can however name certain principles.'

you lure your opponent quickly to play the deep pass into the space behind our defensive line. During that match this happened a lot. By pressuring them in the right way, our defenders generally have one second more time to react and play for the deep pass. At this level this should be sufficient, especially if the back line covering is well organised. The quality of Colombia was that both of the stoppers were capable of providing a quick pass over a long distance to Falcao going deep, causing the ball again to end up perfectly in the space behind our defensive line. This required the utmost from our defenders, but Cillessen as a goalkeeper was very good in covering that space.

Playing in such a daring manner requires a lot of work mentally as well. This starts with the forwards. They can't afford to have a mourning moment after a missed chance or a bad cross. The forwards also need to make the pitch small immediately when the opposition has possession, and decide whether or not they apply

pressure to the ball carrier. Attackers sometimes tend to fail in this. And also in the Dutch national team the types of midfielders like Sneijder, Van der Vaart and Maher; are three fantastic footballers, but they insufficiently understand what work they have to put in for the team when we don't have possession of the ball. This makes a good execution of our daring concept even more complex than it already is. And then it's up to the coach to make choices. Because I've already said that it's especially Van der Vaart who has made it possible that we scored so much from set pieces. Thus, we continuously make choices, because it's always a dynamic whole and the context of every match keeps changing. And there's always that relationship with the qualities of the opposition. For instance, during the game in October 2012 versus Germany (0-0) we decided to let Vermeer make his debut. I was made fun of by some journalists, when I've explained that we preferred a line keeper that time, because the Germans simply like to shoot from distance. During the game, however, that prediction came out, which made Vermeer able to distinguish himself and we kept a clean sheet in that game.

Another example is that compared to Jetro and Willems, Daley Blind performs better when it comes to building up play, but Jetro is a better in the air and is faster. These are all qualities, which you see coming back in our profile sketch for a full back. Then it's up to us as staff to consider whether to search for an even more complete full back who fits our vision and profile sketch better. Or that we will make a choice between the two during the World Cup, partially based on the qualities of the opposition. And like that I could give an example for every position."

THE STRENGTH OF THE NETHERLANDS

What is currently the biggest strength of the Dutch national team?

Louis van Gaal: "At this moment, the Netherlands are at their most dangerous if the opposition is still disorganised when they lose the ball. The acceleration in the positive transition (defence to attack) is our strongest weapon at this point. We've already scored 11 times during those types of situations. This can also be credited to our choice to keep choosing the same types of players who can play the ball deep very well, resulting in consciously selecting the type of forwards like Lens, Narsingh and Robben. This can also be tracked back to the profile sketches of these positions.

But the things that made the Dutch football philosophy famous - the positional play and the build-up from the back - the implementation of this hasn't been good enough so far. This starts with our goalkeepers, who have to make better choices. There are also improvements that can be made by players making themselves available and especially the cross field ball (switching play) as well. First luring the opposition by letting the ball circulate very well at a certain part of the pitch and then suddenly switch the play. That's the basis to be able to disorganise an organised defence, because the space is always on the other side. But we don't master this sufficiently and we'll definitely work hard on it during our preparation.

Of course I follow how my successors at Bayern München work, first Yupp Heynckes and then Josep Guardiola. If you look at this team and this season, you can see the influence by the coach in everything.

Guardiola manages to do it again, just like at Barcelona, to let the team play according to his football vision and make players better. He also taught the players to recognise the right moment to switch the play with a long pass and execute this to perfection in combination with a fantastic game discipline when the other team are in possession, even with creative players like Ribéry, Robben and Götze in the eleven. Their type of game is also defined by a well organised build-up from the back, if that's possible. In addition, they also have a plan B when Bayern are put under pressure during the first phase of the build up. I hope to see all of this coming back to the Dutch national team.

You can hardly see that well organised build-up from the back in England, even in top teams like Manchester United or Manchester City. With the Dutch national team, we should only opt for the long ball from the back if we can't get out of the pressure from the opposition during the build-up phase. Against Turkey we've expected this, because they had to win. That's why Cillessen got ordered to play the long ball in the first instance during that game, so they would eventually choose to not apply pressure. To our surprise the Turks chose to not apply 'high' pressure from the very beginning. Therefore, early in the game, Cillessen could make that choice to build up from the back after all."

PREPARATION

In October 2012 you stated that you were looking forward to the preparation period of the World Cup the most, because you could then exert the most influence as a coach. Are you still that optimistic?

Louis van Gaal: "No, it will be in fact very tight. We'll be able to work with the players from the Dutch league for three weeks, but the players playing in other leagues will arrive a week and a half later. I thought I had more time, but that's not the case. It's annoying, because during that period we will also play games. So there is only very little tactical training time left for the group who needs it the most; the players at clubs abroad.

My fellow coaches in the Netherlands generally let their team play in a way I would like the Netherlands to play as well. Therefore, I would have liked to work a bit longer with the Dutch internationals who play abroad."

How Do You Form the Final Squad for the World Cup?

Louis van Gaal: "Perhaps somebody else will join as well if the circumstances ask for it, but right now I don't expect it. The World Cup squad will consist of players I've already selected before, a choice from a so called A-list of around 35 players. Since August 2012 we've invested a lot in the current squad. At the moments we are together, we've been dealing with each other very intensely. More than the players are used to at their clubs. That intensity could never be held for 30 weeks in a row.

In November 2012 I explained to you in detail, how we've explained to our players what our vision is from the very first moment. If we then come together in Noordwijk for a new international match, we first comprehensively evaluate the previous match. We use that moment again to outline what is expected from each player, for each line, position and profile sketch with the same terms. Always refreshing their memory and confronting them based on those terms, supported by video footage. This is repeated during several one-to-one conversations and of course during training when we play 11 v 11. In such a big game, usually during training behind closed doors, we mimic the opposing team, so that everybody proactively thinks about the best solutions to combat the opposition's choices based on our football vision. This way you learn to think about how you have to play football in different situations if you play for the Dutch national team. You'll never manage to make them master a system in just a few weeks and that's why we've been working on it so long and intensively.

To be part of the final squad, each player has to overcome a few obstacles, for instance, the fitness and form thresholds. The time in preparation and in Brazil is too short to invest energy in players who are not fit or are not performing well. I don't have the illusion that we can get players, who are hopelessly out of shape fit again in just a few weeks' time to play at a World Cup under such difficult conditions.

'I'm not a wizard. I'm a normal coach who tries to make players better through rational ways.'

The climate is definitely not in our advantage. There is a lot of distance we have to cover and, in addition, we also choose a style of play which requires a lot of energy. I've seen for myself how difficult the conditions are. The fitness of the players will be a much more significant issue than I've

estimated beforehand. At the final squad selection for the World Cup, therefore, to what extent a player has shown he is willing to adapt to the severe conditions will also definitely play a role. Just like we will assess whether a player will be prepared to accept a role as a substitute in the interest of the team, and at the same time continue to train sharply.

Because of what awaits us in Brazil, the intensity in the preparation will be high in the beginning during training. Of course not the whole week subsequently, nobody is able to do that. We're talking about blocks with sufficient rest in between to allow the body to recover, and then a block again to stimulate the body and increase the threshold. That's how I've trained at AZ and at Bayern as well.

The preparation has three stages before we travel to Brazil: Hoenderloo, Portugal and then again in the Netherlands. I hope that it will be clear in Hoenderloo that we can select enough players from the Dutch league, because they are available throughout the whole preparation. On the other hand, those players from the Dutch league are used to a whole other intensity compared to those playing for English, German or Spanish top teams. With our expert's eye and by using a variety of measuring results, we'll have to make those players fitter but at the same time not exhaust them too much.

Those 23 players during the first week of training will never be the same 23 to join us in Brazil. Thus, for that stage we also select players from the Netherlands U21 team. Because we strive to work towards a match-specific situation, entirely according to the principles of the Dutch football philosophy, even in the training sessions. The group has to be big enough in order to do this. In a 5 v 5 we don't manage to train sufficiently

according to our vision, how we wish to play football. In an 8v8 or 9v9 I can simulate decently how we play, especially if we selected players based on positions at Netherlands U21 with that objective as a starting point. But yeah, when you start to look at all the players who are injured now, then that will be puzzling as well. With that combination, we play a friendly versus Ecuador on the 17th of May (discussed in previous chapter).

Then after only a few days, we are in Portugal, where I will finally have the players who play abroad at my disposal. In reality getting them so late is a tragedy. Also in Portugal I won't train seven days in a row. Even the body of a top player won't be able to handle that, and besides for such players after a tough season, rest is the best remedy. But let's make it clear that a good adoption of the system is just as important as making the players fit.

Luckily, just like at AZ and Bayern München, I can rely on the information about the fitness level of each individual player that exercise physiologist Jos van Dijk can provide me at any given time. I like to leave nothing to chance.

What I also find important during the runup to and during the World Cup, is to provide a regular change of scenery and space to the players in order to see their wives and kids. A player isn't only a footballer, but also a father of his child, husband and lover. And hopefully the last thing goes for their wives as well..."

For the first time during the interview, we see a very relaxed smile on the face of the Netherlands coach. The opponents of the Netherlands are warned:

The Netherlands head coach is on his toes... more than ever before.

CHAPTER SUMMARY AND LOUIS VAN GAAL QUOTES

FORMATIONS

- During his whole career, Louis van Gaal has chosen 4-3-3 as his basic formation. He explains that he likes a three man defence which he has used in club sides before, but it requires a lot of work during training which you do not necessarily get in international football.

However, as we know now van Gaal did train his players to use the 3-5-2 / 3-4-1-2 formation very successfully at the 2014 World Cup in Brazil.

TACTICS

- The most progress for the Dutch national team is being made during the build-up play in the possession phase when the opposition has a good defensive organisation.

- At this moment, the Netherlands are at their most dangerous if the opposition is still disorganised after they lose the ball.

- There's been significant steps in playing compact when the opposition have the ball. The distance between the defensive line and the strikers has to be left as small as possible. Do not exceed more than 20 -25 metres. Also make sure the distance between the defenders does not exceed 15 metres and strive for 5-10 metres depending on the game situation.

- At every back pass of the opposition, van Gaal gets his teams to push forward. If they win the ball, then depth goes above width, because the opposition won't be well organised.

- Cross field ball (switching play)... 'First luring the opposition by letting the ball circulate very well at a certain part of the pitch and then suddenly switch the play. That's the basis to be able to disorganise an organised defence, because the space is always on the other side.'

TRAINING SESSIONS

- 'I like practice and I speak the language that corresponds to it.'

- Playing 11v11 during training... 'In such a big game, usually during training behind closed doors, we mimic the opposing team, so that everybody proactively thinks about the best solutions to combat the opposition's choices

based on our football vision. This way you learn to think about how you have to play football in different situations.'

- When trying to teach, it seems better to identify four key moments and then divide them into stages. This makes it easier to understand for the players. By naming them, you can make the different stages of key moments from the match trainable and easier.

PLAYER AWARENESS

- 'If I go to scout a potential new player for the Netherlands, I specifically pay attention to their sense of awareness. Awareness is not only dependent on the ball and your teammates' positions, but always also the opposition. You can never do something on the pitch without taking into account the opposition.'

To test this van Gaal uses the 5v3 Possession practice shown on *page 53*

- 'If you often play 5v3, you become better in it and you'll see it displayed during the matches.'

THE IMPORTANCE OF RELAXATION

- 'What I also find important during the run- up to and during the World Cup, is to provide a regular change of scenery and space to the players in order to see their wives and kids. A player isn't only a footballer, but also a father of his child, husband and lover. And hopefully the last thing goes for their wives as well...'

CHAPTER 3

How to Manage the Dutch National Team: The Three Assignments

Text: Tjeu Seeverens en Sef Vergoossen

How to Manage the Dutch National Team: The Three Assignments

'We're Going for the Barcelona-Style with Provocative Pressing'

Twelve points out of four games with a goal difference of 13 v 2. A flying start for Louis van Gaal and the Dutch national team in his second stint as the Netherlands head coach. Van Gaal picked out De Voetbaltrainer to give his first big, substantive interview in his new position. 'Because of the target audience of your magazine, my colleague coaches.' Adding the following with a smile, 'Maybe I'll get more intelligent questions asked by journalists who read this story.' Together with an editor, Sef Vergoossen, as one of those colleague coaches, accepted the challenge to have an in-depth interview with the Netherlands coach.

Do you know which question has kept me busiest prior to this interview? Not the style of play, choice of players or match results. No, every time one question arises: Which process has taken place within the group of the Dutch national team since your appointment, which in a relatively very short time led to a situation where

everything is clear to everyone? As Netherlands head coach you did start with a squad which was partially lost after all. The readers of this magazine, yours and my colleagues, are especially interested in that process. How did you manage to get everyone in and around the Dutch national team to be so supportive of your vision so quickly?

Louis van Gaal: "I think the process side is indeed the most interesting perspective. Football is basically always a process if you're a coach/manager. The most important starting point, if you start a new challenge as head coach, is the composition of your staff. Who do you choose and what do you hope to achieve with them? That's the first thing I've been busy with intensely after my appointment as Netherlands coach. And not, just like many people probably expected, thinking about which players should be selected or not. Your staff is the most significant condition to let the players perform

optimally. That's how I've always thought and worked. At Ajax back then, for that time, I had an unprecedented staff of specialists."

STAFF

You became the Netherlands head coach at a time when almost all other coaches entered commitments for the new season. What influence did this have on your choice?

Louis van Gaal: "It was indeed not the most ideal time to compile my staff, but the final results are something to be proud of. All Dutch staff members from my time at Bayern München knew that they would be asked again, because I was satisfied with their work. Ultimately, only Max Reckers (specialist in video analysis), exercise physiologist Jos van Dijk and goalkeeper coach Frans Hoek were available.

Andries Jonker and Marcel Bout already accepted another job elsewhere, but I also told them to seize the opportunity if something interesting comes up, because I will only take on a new job if something really challenging comes up. I had offers on the table each week, but I only spoke with Ajax and Liverpool. So there was a realistic chance that I wouldn't choose any new adventure. Then suddenly the KNVB asked me to lead the Netherlands to the World Cup in Brazil. Of that challenge - being coach of a national team of a World Cup and preferably of Holland - everybody knew that I aspired to that the most. My predecessor, Bert van Marwijk, had an excellent performance with the Dutch national team, but along the way during the just mentioned process some things went wrong between him and the group of players. You have to do something about that as the new Netherlands coach. But all focus and energy was required for composing the staff first."

Did you try to contact Bert van Marwijk during that period?

Louis van Gaal: "No, but we've thought it out well. The chemistry between the staff and the players of the Netherlands isn't determined by the opinion of the former coach, but by the relationships between the squad and the new staff. Moreover, there was no point for me to take a closer look into what happened. If you hear several stories about it, then ultimately you'll pick a side yourself. They are also subjective, because the narrators have been in the middle of that process. Of course we've discussed it with team manager Hans Jorritsma and Kees Jansma about what happened during the European Championship, but always in relation to the direction we wish to reach with the Netherlands in the future."

THREE ASSIGNMENTS

Louis van Gaal: "The KNVB has put the bar very high to reach the last four at the World Cup 2014 in Brazil. You can ask yourself whether that's a realistic goal, however, we're accepting that challenge. During the composition of the staff we've taken into account the assignments given to me by the KNVB. There are three:

1. Playing recognisable football according to the Dutch football philosophy.

2. On our way to Brazil the youth has to be integrated.

3. The Dutch people should be able to identify themselves again with the Dutch national team.

Then it can't be a surprise if you end up with Danny Blind again. As a former top

footballer and captain with Ajax he has won everything that could be won at club level and he has a good history as an international. And then his career as a manager/coach, he has been youth coach, technical manager, assistant coach, head coach, technical director and head of the youth academy under me. A star, even back then. In addition, Blind is also a specialist when it comes to scouting. There is no one with as much knowledge about talented footballers in Holland as him. Also significantly we share the same vision on football. This is a condition for an assistant, otherwise sooner or later there will be friction. You have to present a united vision to the players. But also important, in details our opinions differ a lot and that's the resistance I'm looking for every time as well. Yes-men are useless. Based on their expertise and strong arguments, each staff member should feel free to share another opinion if he thinks that it fits the stated, common vision and framework."

And then next to Danny Blind you chose Patrick Kluivert. For me that wasn't a surprise at all. A few years ago I was a guest speaker at the Coach Course of Professional Football. There, I was told a story about how I had only five days to get the PSV squad behind a common football vision. Of that whole group of participants, Patrick Kluivert made the best impression on me that day. He was already thinking like a mature coach four years ago.

Louis van Gaal: "I of course know Patrick Kluivert very well. He made his debut for Ajax in 1994 under me, played at Barcelona when I was the coach and also for the Dutch national team during my first period as manager. Yes, the development of Patrick as a coach has surprised me. With players like Danny Blind and Frank de Boer you could predict that they would develop themselves well as coaches, because

'Kluivert is the coach from our staff who will communicate our vision with the players the most.'

they've always been thinkers. Patrick was an intuitive footballer and that type of player gets in trouble as a coach more often if he has to operate in an analytical, abstract and process-driven way. Kluivert is an exception to this rule. During my period at AZ he had a traineeship. That's probably around the same time you saw him at the course. It soon became clear how good he was in bringing his story across to an individual player. Thus, it would only be a matter of time and development when he would also be capable to convey this story to a group.

We can also see what he's prepared to sacrifice to succeed as a coach. Don't forget, Kluivert is the former football player who came immediately as a striker after big names like Cruyff and Van Basten. This doesn't stop him, however, from choosing

the hardest path. First to NEC and now young FC Twente, weaker teams than he could have chosen to coach in professional football. You only have a small core of players at your disposal during training sessions and you also have to deal with less motivated players for the first time during the matches, and on the other hand very young U18 talents. Yet Patrick deliberately chose to enter that path and became champions with that team. It's unfathomable that there is so little appreciation for this. Especially because the 36-year old Kluivert knows exactly what he should have done differently during his career as a player. Either way, I'm very pleased with Patrick. The current generation of internationals has seen him play themselves and he speaks their language. Therefore, Kluivert is the coach from our staff who will communicate our vision with the players the most. In that area I have complete trust in Patrick. That's also a conscious choice in relation to the assignment given by the KNVB to rejuvenate the squad.

In a different way this also goes for Piet Bon, the experienced practitioner from the staff. He's also able to devote attention to the sports psychology aspects. He is a wise man with a lot of empathy, who also participated in the rowing competition at the Olympic level. Ideal as a counsellor in a sort of father figure way for the team, Piet is just present. If you need him as a player, he's always available. Some players will need it more often than others, and there will also be players who have no need for it. It's important that you know that there's someone for you if you could use some additional support on the mental aspect. In addition, we as a staff can always make use of a team of sports psychologists, because that has been available for years for me in the background if the process requires it."

FITNESS

Now that we're talking about practitioner Piet Bon, I remember one of your quotes that you'll only select fit players for the Dutch national team. That will also have consequences for the composition of your staff.

Louis van Gaal: "Absolutely. That's why I chose a comprehensive medical staff. I saw sports physician Edwin Goedhart working for the very first time in 2001 in Argentina during the U19 World Cup. I then brought him in as a doctor at AZ, then he became head of the medical staff at Ajax and now he works in the same position at Vitesse. His knowledge isn't limited to the medical world. He also knows a lot about communication and management. He's involved with the "Team Performance Exchange". This is the online communication platform for our staff and the players, which we once introduced at AZ and now at the KNVB. We use it to inform the group of players with messages but also with video footage. The system makes it possible for us to compose a portfolio, to offer specific studies or collect other data. Each member of staff and squad has a personal login and password. Gijs van Heumen is the facilitator of that system. As former coach of the Dutch national hockey team, he knows from experience which information you would like to share with your players or wish to collect.

The presence of a good orthopedist in the staff is a necessity, because most of the football injuries are caused by the locomotor system of a player. For that position, Edwin chose Rien Heijboer of the Rotterdam Erasmus MC. In the past he guided top athletes of various disciplines and he's specialised in knee ligament injuries. Regarding the Physiotherapy

*René Wormhoudt **(behind Danny Blind) has been added to the staff as the fitness and conditioning coach.***

department, we've chosen most of the staff that was functioning under Bert van Marwijk as well, because the players were familiar with them. We've only added René Wormhoudt as a rehabilitation coach."

'Fitness also means mental fitness'

Louis van Gaal: "When I'm speaking of fitness, I'm not only talking about physical fitness. The mental fitness is just as important. Players who are distracted by other issues, do not meet that criterion. During my first term as Netherlands coach I sometimes selected a player in order to let him gain confidence. You can think like

that as a club manager, but not as a coach of the national team. At the Dutch national team only the direct results during the match is what always counts, and at this level you can only achieve that with players who are 100% fit. For a team to be successful the input of each player is needed, unless your name is Messi. We don't have a player of his calibre yet, regardless of how talented some players are. Maybe there will be one who comes close to the level of Messi, but right now that's not the case. Therefore, no one is irreplaceable and that's why you have to be 100% fit every time you report to the Netherlands. We don't reserve any time and space to offer players the possibility to

The Three Assignments:

1. To play recognisable football according to the Dutch football philosophy

2. Integrate young players into the World Cup squad

3. The Dutch people should be able to identify themselves with the Dutch national team

recover from an injury around a match of the Dutch national team, because they happen to want to be part of the group. But we are not there yet as a staff. We've also maintained a few people from the staff from Bert van Marwijk, partially at the request of the KNVB and of course because I'm convinced about their abilities.

For instance, team manager Hans Jorritsma who's been playing that role since 1996 to the satisfaction of each coach and that also applied for me during my first stint. If Jorritsma takes care of something, it's really taken care of. The contract with Kees Jansma as press officer has been extended for two years as well. He's a qualified professional with whom I had a disagreement with in the past one time. What I've always appreciated about him, is that it never had an impact on our relationship from his side. It's been well known for years that Monique Kessels and Martiene Bruggink (from the PR staff) have been functioning well, which also applies to Maaike Voorbergen, the management assistant of the technical staff.

Good scouting is essential for a coach of a national team. I have my own ideas about it, which I've processed into a scouting form during my first stint as Netherlands coach. But you know how it goes; once you're gone, such a form and thereby the vision on scouting disappears in a drawer or even the archive. Now it's out again. Ronald Spelbos, the chief scout under my predecessors, looked at players in a different way and not based on my profile sketches for each position and line. On the other hand Ronald of course is an experienced professional, whose expertise is very useful. At my request now, besides Ronald, Edward Metgod also focuses on the scouting. Edward
knows and shares my vision on scouting.

The KNVB accepted my request to change his part-time job into a job with full availability."

Scout7

Edward Metgod is a specialist when it comes to working with Scout7, the best player tracking system in the world.

Louis van Gaal: "The data file contains information about more than 100,000 players and any information about 126 competitions in 60 countries, spread over the whole world. Since 2009 it's possible to search through the application Scout7Xeatre as a subscriber, each competition weekend, to choose from 1600 full matches and look at interesting players, matches or tournaments. Through a live stream on the internet those selected games can be followed easily in the living room. By linking this with the data systems like Opta and Amisco we're capable of requesting certain information next to the selected footage. This way you can compare the performance and statistical data of our internationals. On a timeline you can see if the movement pattern of a player during a match has changed or observe if a player keeps losing the ball during a specific phase of the match or in a specific situation. You can also easily map the accuracy level of passing or the number of times a player is involved in the build-up. This type of information can then easily be shared with the players through the Team Performance website, supported by footage."

LINE-UP

The most interesting question is, what do you guys do with all this data?

Louis van Gaal: "That's what it's all about

of course. Bert van Marwijk composed a list with around 50 players, which are or will be eligible for the Dutch national team now or in the future. It would have been strange if we, as technical staff, didn't use this list as a starting point to determine the order for each position within the formation 4-3-3 in two different variants; with 1 defensive midfielder or 2 defensive midfielders. Also, we have the option for the 3-4-3 formation if the opposition plays with two strikers. At this level there are very few players who can be used in multiple positions. In a weekend, the scouts and assistants usually watch a few games live. They use those moments to have contact with the internationals as well, because this can't just stay restricted to international matches. In addition, each weekend there is a selection of footage and data made with Scout7.

There is also a group of scouts active, working on a pro bono basis, because they like to do that type of work for me. The findings of all that data is used by Danny Blind, exercise physiologist Jos van Dijk, goalkeeper coach Frans Hoek and the scouts Ronald Spelbos and Edward Metgod every Monday to determine whether the order for each position should change based on all up-to-date data. So basically they design a new lineup each time within our system, with the best order of the players for each position. On Tuesday the results of that preliminary consultation get discussed with me. The other staff members then have to convince me if they think that the order on a certain position should change. Afterwards, we know all together what's currently the strongest possible Dutch national team and who's in form and who isn't. The closer the next match gets, the more we take into account the specific abilities of the upcoming opponent with that line-up form. The final squad eventually, once

again, is the result of a logical process whereby nothing is left to chance."

How many games do you watch live in football stadiums?

Louis van Gaal: "Not too many anymore. If you decide to attend a game, it usually requires a lot of travelling time. At the same time there is always a match on television with our internationals playing, in Holland as well as abroad. Therefore, it's more effective to make a selection of games on TV for the weekend, which enables you to look at as many potential internationals as possible. Usually this is around 75% of the squad."

DIVISION OF TASKS

What's the allocation of tasks within the technical staff in the periods preceding the match?

Louis van Gaal: "I only stand in front of the group if it's about the total picture of our tactical preparation. That's who I coach, the first eleven, if we simulate the upcoming match on the pitch in an 11v11 situation. Patrick Kluivert assists me in this case. Danny Blind, who knows everything about the opposition thanks to the information and footage from Metgod and Spelbos, coaches the eleven reserves and gives them assignments which have a link with the style of play of that particular opponent. Danny Blind also discusses the opposition during the pre-match talk and Frans Hoek takes care of the set pieces. On the day of the match we pay a lot of attention to line discussions (separating the players into their specific positions to have detailed discussions as defensive, midfield and forward lines). In duration and form these discussions differ for each line, because the defenders can usually process information

better and more than midfielders and in turn they can process more than forwards, even if you use footage.

I take care of the line discussions myself and with the forwards I get supported by Kluivert, while Danny Blind helps me with the midfielders and defenders. With each individual player, it depends on the position of the player which of the two assistants is present."

THE HOTEL REQUIREMENTS

And then the first squad selection...

Louis van Gaal: "No! I've first reviewed the regular players' hotel of the Netherlands; Huis ter Duin in Noordwijk. The internationals, until then were sleeping spread over three floors. I want the whole squad to have a room on the same floor. Also, it's important that the medical room is placed on a central location of that floor. Furthermore, I wanted to create a sort of hall near the medical room where the players of the Netherlands could have fun and communicate freely with each other. In other words, it's about creating conditions which make players decide to do something together if there is any time for it in the programme. They can, for instance, play cards, watch TV, play games, participate in that famous ice hockey game or play table tennis. There are always around fifteen or sixteen players present.

'Huis ter Duin (team hotel) has been renovated on my request'

All my wishes have been met. The renovation in the hotel was completed before the first qualification match against Turkey. The details play an important role for me then as well. For example, the internet connection was too slow for players who play video games and that causes unnecessary irritation. We experienced the same issues as a staff when we wanted to request and share the footage of analysis in a quick way. Now the internet connection is functioning perfectly."

PRE-MATCH PLANNING

Louis van Gaal: "And then it was time to start thinking about the squad for the friendly match against Belgium. This hardly cost me any time. I've personally only introduced Bruno Martins Indi, from Feyenoord, because he left a good impression on me during the game against Dynamo Kiev in the qualifying round of the Champions League. Then of course, we've also had to deal with the core of the squad from Van Marwijk, and for the rest I had complete faith in the knowledge of Danny Blind regarding the best talents in the Netherlands. Much more time and energy has been invested in the meticulous preparation on the first days we were together with this squad in the run-up to Belgium. That first time is such an important moment in that process, which made me, more than ever before, leave nothing to chance. Every step, each action is well thought out in advance. During the thinking process I write everything about it for myself. What am I going to say? What is the correct order? When do I say something and against whom? Which tone do I use at which moment? What's the right sphere and environment for each activity? How do I vary my interaction with the group of players? When do I let my assistants speak to the group? What's the best order for individual conversations? How and at what time do I choose my captains? Which supporting footage do I use and which

space is the most suitable to do this? How do I channel the expected media attention? But let's go through the programme in the days before Belgium, then my approach becomes even clearer.

DESIRE

After the European Championships it was clear that there were a lot of old issues in the core of the Dutch national team. The stories about it were all over the media. Everybody could read, see and hear that the relationship between some players was disrupted. As a new coach you usually take the decision to start with a group discussion to overcome these problems. That would have been logical this time as well, but we've deliberately chosen not to. I've asked myself the question; What drives these players, despite all mutual frustrations, to report themselves to the Dutch national team again? Why do I want to be the coach of the Netherlands so bad? Apparently there has to be something which unites us. I think the answer is that I have a desire to achieve the maximum results by playing good football at the highest level. And then it was all clear to me that we're starting with amazing footage of the Netherlands from the past few years.

Then of course the players could say something like: 'Barcelona is club football. Those players train every day to perfect the execution. At a national team this isn't possible and therefore we'll never reach that level.' That's why the players immediately afterwards have been shown footage of Spain who play with the Barcelona-style in mind, but with some subtle changes. This also applies to me. On important details, especially in the final stage, my vision about what's attractive and effective, and what will be appreciated more by the Dutch people, differs slightly. Then we're talking about one of those basic assignments again. I've added verbal comments to the visuals of Barcelona and Spain. What did I like about it and at which moments in a match will we make different decisions?

We've also explained why we have a preference for a 4-3-3 style of play with one deep lying player (defensive midfielder) instead of two. Afterwards the players have been sent back to their rooms. Then what any coach likes to happen automatically happens when the players visualise and imagine what they've heard and seen during the first meeting in their beds."

THE BARCELONA STYLE OF PLAY

Furthermore, footage has been shown about my football vision and of the staff to play football in the Barcelona style.

'This is the most difficult style, but that's what we're aiming for with this group.'

'I decided to base the choice for a new captain and vice-captain on the roundtable discussion.'

MEDIA

Louis van Gaal: "In the afternoon we chose to have a fun training session with lots of 'piggy in the middle' possession games led by Danny Blind and Patrick Kluivert. I've postponed the necessary roundtable discussion until after dinner. After such a first training session, there is always a moment of contact by the players with the media. It was predictable that the journalists especially wanted to know all that has been said that morning. Of course they expected to hear about a session where the differences were settled, but were now instead dealing with players who could only tell that they've spoken about the football vision in a good way. The result of a well thought choice regarding the order of the activities on that first day. If you don't think about it very well in advance, you'll most likely have a serious problem in that moment.

SELECTING A CAPTAIN

There was another issue that day. After the 'farewell' of Mark van Bommel, a new captain had to be appointed. This could easily have led to a source of unrest. I myself was still uninhibited and didn't have a preference beforehand. So I decided to base the choice for a new captain and vice-captain on the roundtable discussion. However, beforehand, that was still an uncertain factor. The players first had to decide whether staff could be present during that conversation. Before the discussion would take place, we thought about which players should be invited. There were some players who didn't get selected for the European Championship or didn't get any playing time. During such a discussion, the group can't be too big. Therefore, the condition was that only players who played at the European Championship were there (13 of the 23 players).

For that important conversation I've chosen a space in Huis ter Duin, which would be most suitable in relation to the atmosphere. A nice room with a fireplace. I've let someone adjust the lighting. The chairs of the players were positioned in a semi-circle, so everybody could look each other in the face. Behind those chairs, the chairs of other staff members were placed, and in front of that circle a chair and desk was placed for me. Of course I've initiated that meeting and again I've used visuals.

COMMUNICATING WITH PLAYERS

For that special occasion I chose to show a part of an episode of "Andere Tijden Sport"which was broadcast in June 2010. The episode is about everything that happened during the European Championship in 1996 under Guus Hiddink, and what he did afterwards to turn the 1998 World Cup campaign into an amazing tournament two years later. New rules and agreements about how you want to treat each other played a big role back then. A nice detail is that Patrick Kluivert also shows up in that episode and he was in that room at that moment. After that footage we also showed a few visuals of the successful World Cup in South Africa and an interview with Wesley Sneijder just before the previous European Championship. Therein he stated that a Dutch national team with so many qualities could only be aiming for the title. Subsequently I've only added the following: 'How is it possible that it turned out differently? That's what the coming roundtable discussion is about. It's up to you guys whether we may be present.' The team told us we could stay and that of course is pleasant, because this immediately expresses trust. Every coach then knows that there will be players who will be saying something, players who keep quiet and players who show what they think by using their body language. This time wasn't different from the norm. It became a conversation that lasted almost two hours, the contents of which I obviously won't discuss. What goes for the players also goes for the staff.

After the roundtable discussion I also presented my rules to the group in a sort of manifest. This was well suited for the beginning of the meeting and the documentary about 1996/1998. Obviously I've discussed my rules with the other staff members first. They've made some additions, but also erased a few things. Therefore, we could present a version which each staff member agreed with. These rules were also supported by visuals. For example, the YouTube clip 'Headphones' of Sporting Telenet was shown prior to the agreements made about wearing headphones. In the clip various top athletes are kind of mocked while shown wearing headphones.

The agreements made apply to everyone and it's the intention that we correct each other if someone does not honour them, whether it's a player or a staff member. The players saw that starting point back in the video clip wherein a son tries to find something in the refrigerator in the middle of the night, and suddenly discovers that his mother came home late and secretly carries shoes in her hands while walking up the stairs. The mother subsequently gets put in her place by her son. The players council was informed that my door was always open if the group has a different opinion about a certain rule. We could then always talk about it. Like I said before, I've also used the roundtable discussion to choose my captains. That same evening Wesley Sneijder and Dirk Kuijt were invited for a conversation. Both of them accepted

their new role. I've explained to them what responsibilities it entails and we've also talked about standards and values. This was all on Day 1…"

STRUCTURE

Louis van Gaal: "The day after was partially devoted to the comments from the group on everything that happened the night before in relation to the group dynamic. We woke up at 9:15 and that will also be the case in the coming international matches. My preference goes out to fixed intervals, or in other words a recognisable structure in the daily rhythm. The players shouldn't have to look at a piece of paper to find out when they have to wake up, train, have lunch or rest. What's also important is the principle 'always easy, never rush'.

'Always Easy, Never Rush'

After breakfast, the first individual conversations were held. First with Robin van Persie, because he wouldn't play against Belgium. That conversation originally was planned on the first day after the roundtable discussion, but Van Persie then thought it was becoming late and that's why we've rescheduled it to the second day. After Van Persie we spoke to Arjen Robben because he wouldn't play on the right, like at Bayern München, but on the left. Normally this would have been two intensive conversations, but we were on the same line very quickly. Sometimes not everything can be explained perfectly, and you base the choice for a player on your gut feeling. It was important that these conversations took place before the 11 v 11 training session and the pre-match discussion before Belgium. If you choose the wrong order at such moments, then the

effect of a successful roundtable discussion could get partially lost."

ROTATION

Then the qualifiers came up and you're probably the first coach of the national team to rotate his players a lot when two international matches in just a few days were scheduled. Do you then take into account beforehand that you don't want to win against Andorra with 6-0 but with 3-0, because you want to win the game against Romania per se afterwards?

Louis van Gaal: "What you're saying now, I don't believe a word of that. Just review the footage of the match against Andorra once again. We could have won with the Dutch national team by 6-0 as well. Many opportunities weren't converted, penalties unjustifiably didn't get awarded, and a goal got disallowed…

Against Andorra we played with that specific team, because of my opinion that one striker is better in the box than the other and that one winger is better in small spaces. I also explain this to all of the players, sometimes during a pre-match discussion and at other times in a personal conversation. 'This is why I've chosen you and that's what I want to see coming back on the pitch.' Always providing that clarity. And if a player doesn't show it during the next training session, then I'm very alert to it. 'I've just told you why I chose you and now you don't show it on the pitch. Or am I seeing this the wrong way?'"

MOTIVATION

Do you consider that correcting or motivating?

'Everything I say is intended to motivate players.'

Louis van Gaal: "Everything I say is intended to motivate players. They need to strive to be even better as a footballer. That's also the starting point of every evaluation. As coach of the national team it's an easier part of your job than for a coach of a club, but still equally important. At Bayern München I evaluated the progress of the process with my players, usually two or three times a week. Then you have to think even more about the tone, number of times, duration and form, otherwise they drift away. With the players of the Dutch national team I obviously have less evaluation time, but that's also something players are still not looking forward to. Danny, Patrick and I then usually say it like it is, but we've told the players; 'Don't consider it as personal criticism, but as us reaching out to help you become an even better football player.' I inform every new player in the squad on which grounds I selected him, in relation to

the position I have in mind for him in the team. The latter is important to mention. Gertjan Verbeek was apparently mad when we told Maher in such a conversation that we would like him to function as a number 10, while he played as a right midfielder at AZ at that time. Within the system that AZ applies, and considering the players Verbeek had at his disposal, it was understandable that he was positioned on the right of the midfield at his club. But at the Dutch national team we're dealing with other players. Therefore, it's possible that we as a staff use the qualities of a player for a different position than he's used to at his club."

But what if Alex Ferguson decided all of a sudden to permanently play Van Persie on the left, would that have any consequences for him regarding his position as a striker in the Dutch national team?

'Against Andorra we applied pressure everywhere on the pitch, because we knew that we would gain possession back again rapidly.'

Louis van Gaal: "At that moment you have to consider that amongst your coaching team. It's conceivable that Van Persie would be positioned on the left in our weekly line-up form in such a situation as well. On that position, he then gets compared to other players. But that's not relevant now and I don't really like those types of speculations. I leave that to the media."

STYLE OF PLAY

I would like to know a bit more about the style of play and the choices you make. Is it correct when I say that you let the defensive block push backwards a bit further than van Marwijk when the opposition have possession?

Louis van Gaal: "Yes, and I do this because that choice fits the qualities of this group of players the best. We first create space to make optimal use of the speed of players

like Lens, Robben, Narsingh, Schaken and Van Persie. The proof got delivered, as weird as that may sound, against Andorra. We applied pressure everywhere on the pitch because we knew that we would win back possession again rapidly. In the end it didn't yield too much. Against a stronger Romanian side we first created the space and afterwards, we profited from the speed of our forwards. This proved to be a lot more effective. That's how I've played with AZ as well for four years, but it was hardly recognised. Everybody said we purely played attacking football, but that wasn't the case. We played attractive football when we had possession with quick and deep movement, but also at AZ we had to first create conditions to make this possible when the opposition had possession of the ball.

That's also the subtle change I would like to apply with the Dutch national team to the

'Against a stronger Romanian side we first created the space and afterwards, we profited from the speed of our forwards. I call that provocative pressing.'

Barcelona style. The ball circulation at Barcelona is perfectly executed on a technical level, but it's way too broad. The ball gets played 10 yards forwards diagonally, at most, and then often back or wide towards the other side of the pitch.

In my opinion, you should skip more stations and the ball should go way more towards the opposition's goal. This is only possible if you first 'provoke' that space and subsequently use it for those quick movements in depth. For the spectators it's much more pleasant to watch.

'Provocative pressing is my subtle change to the Barcelona-style'

Barcelona want to gain possession as quickly as possible, therefore, they press very early, but at the same time they only create a very small space to function. If you don't want to lose possession then you need to automatically play the ball wide or back more often. For the supporters in the stands that's less enjoyable to watch. And with that we end up at one of those assignments again, which the KNVB gave us; the Dutch people must be able to identify themselves again with the Dutch national team. That's what our style of play fits to right now. This gets picked up quickly, because there are mainly positive comments from the supporters about the way we've played during our qualification matches. And we've been together on our journey for two months."

MIDFIELD

Remarkable for this Netherlands team is the way in which the midfield operates. They keep anticipating new situations by rotating or tilting. Sometimes you see two players in front of the defence, then at other times you only see one. Which agreements have been made about that?

Louis van Gaal: "That has everything to do with the qualities of Kevin Strootman. Trust me, he's a star. He's the key for a balanced Dutch national team in the midfield. He does this based on his gut feeling, but even then he almost always makes the right decision."

And do the rest adapt themselves to him?

Louis van Gaal: "Strootman adapts himself to the game, to what's needed at that point. Strootman also makes it possible that we can play with one deep lying midfielder more easily. That's how he wishes to play himself as well. But yes, Kevin is also a box-to-box player with an exceptional ability to cover huge distances. If Leroy Fer soon becomes fit again, then we will have another similar type of player in the Dutch squad. However, he still has to prove this on the highest level. In today's modern football, these types of players play a crucial role. But within a team you also require three or four creative players. In some top matches, using four of such players is a little bit too much, possibly causing the team to be unbalanced."

Do you want Van der Vaart to end up on the right and left side?

Louis van Gaal: "No, he's a creative player who can make a difference. You have to allow him to play where his preference lies, and with Van der Vaart that's on the right."

FOCUS

After the victory against Romania everybody said 'This can't go wrong anymore.' How do you make sure there is still sufficient focus?

Louis van Gaal: "For myself this isn't a problem because of the intensive way I prepare for each match, together with my staff. Usually you also pass this on to the players. In addition, as Netherlands coach I can substitute a player more easily and quicker than a club manager if one or more players aren't involved enough anymore. Nobody has to be afraid that we'll lose our concentration, because we're not there just yet and the objective for everybody has to be to become better as a team."

SEF VERGOOSSEN'S CONCLUSION

"After conducting this interview with Louis van Gaal, for me, it's clear now how the process was conducted to turn a divided group into a squad with natural discipline and commitment about the common vision and route in such a short time."

CHAPTER SUMMARY AND LOUIS VAN GAAL QUOTES

STAFF

- Louis van Gaal believes the most important starting point, if you start a new challenge as a head coach, is the composition of your staff.

- 'Yes-men are useless. Based on their expertise and strong arguments, each staff member should feel free to share another opinion if he thinks that it fits the stated, common vision and framework.'

- 'The players and staff have to speak the same football language regardless.'

- 'Obviously I've discussed my rules with the other staff members first. They've made some additions, but also erased a few things. Therefore, we could present a version which each staff member agreed with. These rules were also supported by visuals.'

THE THREE ASSIGNMENTS

1. Playing recognisable football according to the Dutch football philosophy.

2. On our way to Brazil the youth has to be integrated.

3. The Dutch people should be able to identify themselves again with the Dutch national team.

FITNESS

- Mental fitness is as important as physical fitness.

- Every Netherlands player on the pitch has to be 100% fit for the team to achieve their goals. There is only an exception here if you have a player like Messi.

SCOUTING AND VIDEO ANALYSIS

- Louis van Gaal and his coaches use video analysis and scout reports to discuss the best players based on performance for the current playing system his team is using.

After this they know the current strongest possible Dutch team and who's in form and who isn't.

MAN MANAGEMENT

- Louis van Gaal often uses an open process to make big decisions, taking into account the views of his staff and players to make big decisions - 'I've also used the roundtable discussion to choose my captains.'

- His door is always open to his players who want to discuss anything with him. He also has individual talks with his players to tell them what he expects before and after matches:

  'This is why I've chosen you and that's what I want to see coming back on the pitch.'

  'I've just told you why I chose you and now you don't show it on the pitch. Or am I seeing this the wrong way?'

- It is important to make the rules clear to all players in a group environment.

- Everything van Gaal says to his players is intended to motivate them. He informs every new player on which grounds he selected him, in relation to the position he has in mind.

- 'Sometimes not everything can be explained perfectly, and you base the choice for a player on your gut feeling.'

CHAPTER 4

Louis van Gaal Netherlands Training Practices 2012-2014

PRACTICE FORMAT

Each practice includes clear diagrams with supporting training notes such as:

- Name of Practice
- Objective of Practice
- Description of Practice
- Variation or Progression (if applicable)
- Coaching Points
- Louis van Gaal's Instructions (if applicable)

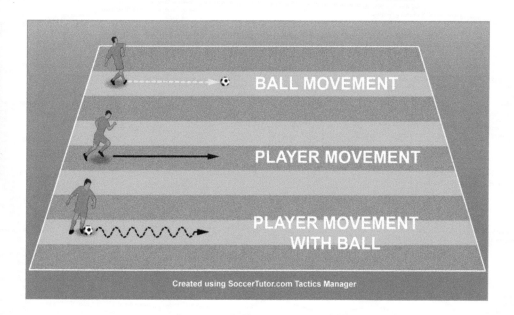

BALL MOVEMENT

PLAYER MOVEMENT

PLAYER MOVEMENT
WITH BALL

Created using SoccerTutor.com Tactics Manager

LOUIS VAN GAAL NETHERLANDS TRAINING PRACTICES 2012-2014

De Voetbaltrainer attended several training sessions of the Netherlands in September and October of 2012.

At least three times we saw a popular basic drill, namely 'the Triangle' (see the next 3 training practices). Behind the simple looking drill, a complete philosophy is hidden.

Following the interviews, we can now give a good insight to the readers about Louis van Gaal's actual way of working in training.

We also saw training at Quick Boys in Katwijk, at the training accommodation in Hoenderloo, in various stadiums across Europe, during the 2014 training camp in Lagos (Portugal) and in Brazil during the World Cup.

Of course, we saw many of the same types of training back, but the methodological progress was thought out and the coaching moments were increasingly detailed and demanding. We also saw the implementation of a number of training methods in particular and saw vast improvements over the months.

PASSING + DRIBBLE COMBINATION 'TRIANGLE'

We may perhaps call the 'Triangle' the most basic form of the basic shapes when it comes to Louis van Gaal. This basic technique of passing over a maximum of 10/15 yards, the pressure from fast ball speed and training players to be two-footed (left and right, compulsory left or right touch) are all central to this form of training.

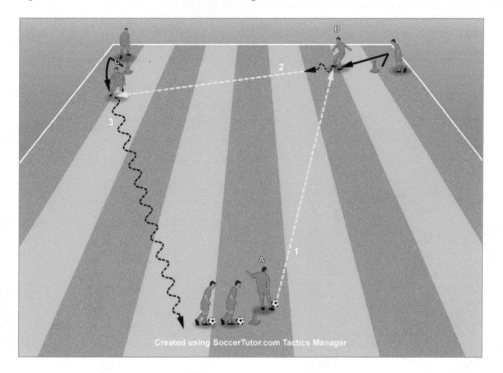

Objective
To develop quick, short to medium rage accurate passing, creating space, timing and rhythm.

Description
We mark out a triangle with 3 cones 10-15 yards apart and use a minimum of 6/7 players.

Player A passes to Player B who checks away from the cone, receives, takes a touch and then passes across for Player C (who also checks away) to run onto. To finish the sequence Player C dribbles the ball to the start position.

Each player moves to the next position (A -> B -> C) and the next player in line starts a new sequence. When a mistake gets made during the drill, everybody still keeps moving to the next position, to keep the rhythm of this exercise. Change the direction of play often.

Coaching Points

1. The movement away from the cone has to be made explosively (in a game situation you have to break free from your opponent). The movement has to be made just before the teammate passes the ball, basically at the last second.

2. Always receive with the back foot (foot furthest away from the ball).

3. There should be continuous movement without the ball.

4. Speed of play should be high, with the technical execution aligned to the style of play.

5. Players have to challenge each other, demand the utmost from one another; thereby mistakes are no problem, however as a condition, the concentration needs to be optimal.

Louis van Gaal's Instructions

- "Make space to receive the ball."
- "Pass the ball to your teammate's strongest foot."
- "Timing, rhythm in the exercise."
- "Discipline in your head every time, accurate passes."
- "Coach together. Ask for the ball."
- "All over the ground."

PROGRESSION **DOUBLE ONE-TWO COMBINATION TRIANGLE**

In his progression we have a 'Double Triangle' with one-two combinations. We saw this training practice the day before the memorable 5-1 win over Spain at the World Cup. There was, of course, a high degree of automation/routine in the execution. The players could train attuned to one another and one word was enough to communicate.

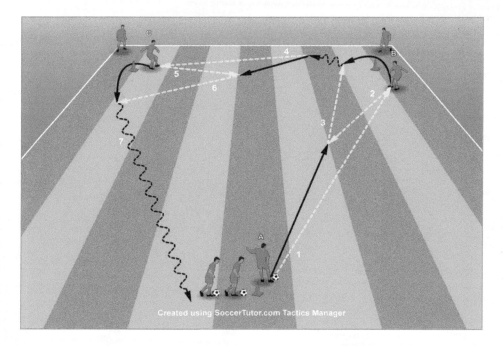

Description

In this progression we add 1-2 combinations. Player A plays a 1-2 combination with Player B who runs around the cone (as shown) to receive the pass back. Player B then plays a 1-2 combination with Player C who runs around the cone to receive the pass back and finishes the sequence by dribbling the ball to the start position.

Each player moves to the next position (A -> B -> C) and the next player in line starts a new sequence. When a mistake gets made during the drill, everybody still keeps moving to the next position, to keep the rhythm in this exercise. Change the direction of play often.

Coaching Points

1. The pass back needs to be in front of the player so they can play a one touch pass.

2. The players need quick and light feet to run around the cone and meet the pass.

3. It is important that the player moves around the first cone as quickly as possible (accelerates). The other player has to anticipate this by adjusting the speed of the pass.

4. Player C should not automatically accelerate, but should adjust the speed around the second cone as the timing is very important.

VARIATION **DOUBLE ONE-TWO COMBINATION TRIANGLE (2)**

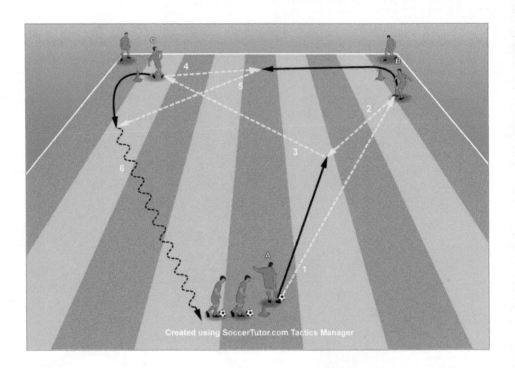

Created using SoccerTutor.com Tactics Manager

Description
In this variation we change the passing combination slightly. Player A plays a 1-2 combination with Player B and then passes to Player C (as shown). Player B runs all the way around and Player C then plays a 1-2 combination with Player B. Player C moves around the cone to receive the pass back on the run and finishes the sequence by dribbling the ball to the start position.

Each player moves to the next position (A -> B -> C) and the next player in line starts a new sequence. When a mistake gets made during the drill, everybody still keeps moving to the next position, to keep the rhythm in this exercise. Change the direction of play often.

Conclusion
The 'triangle' as a passing combination drill has deliberately been chosen because of the fact that a triangle keeps recurring in player positioning on the pitch in multiple systems such as the 4-3-3, 3-4-3, 4-4-1-1 (diamond) or the 4-4-2 (diamond)

The triangle shows the passing lines and choices (good for decision making). Then afterwards the players can recognise this and apply it during match-specific situations.

PASSING 'SQUARE' - RECEIVE, DIRECTIONAL TOUCH, PASS AND FOLLOW

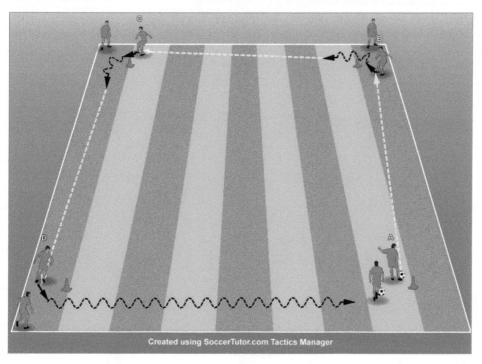

Created using SoccerTutor.com Tactics Manager

Objective
To develop passing, receiving and dribbling at high speed.

Description
In a 10-15 yard square, players are in groups of 8.

Start with 1 ball and Player A passes to Player B who receives, takes the ball around the cone and passes to Player C. Player C receives and takes the ball around the cone, before passing to Player D who does the same.

To complete the sequence, Player D dribbles to the start position. Each player moves to the next position (A -> B -> C -> D) and the next player in line starts a new sequence. Run this exercise in both directions.

Coaching Points

1. Players need to check away and then move to meet the pass.

2. Players should receive the ball with their back foot (foot furthest away from the ball).

3. The players should also be side on when receiving with an open body shape.

PROGRESSION PASSING 'SQUARE' - TIMING OF MOVEMENT IN A QUICK ONE-TWO COMBINATION DRILL

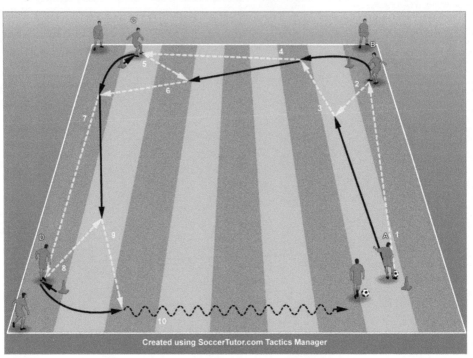

Created using SoccerTutor.com Tactics Manager

Objective

To develop one-two combinations and player movement (timing) at high speed.

Description

In this progression, we introduce one-two combinations at each cone.

Player A passes to Player B, moves forward to receive the pass back and passes into the space in front of the cone. Player B times his movement around the cone to receive the pass back. Player B then plays a 1-2 combination with Player C, who then does the same with Player D.

Player D finishes the sequence by dribbling to the start position. Each player moves to the next position (A -> B -> C -> D) and the next player in line starts a new sequence. Run this practice in both directions.

Coaching Points

1. The timing of the movement is key to the rhythm of this drill.

2. Passes need to be correctly weighted and timed for the movement around the cone.

VARIATION TIMING OF MOVEMENT IN A QUICK ONE-TWO COMBINATION DRILL WITH THIRD MAN RUN

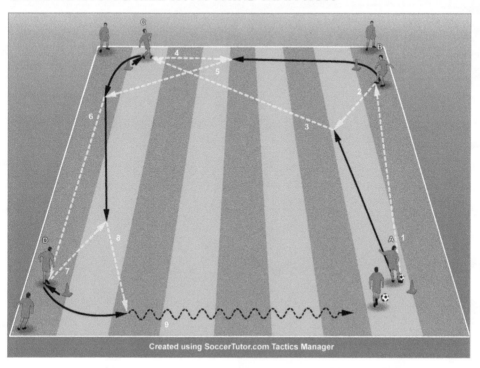

Created using SoccerTutor.com Tactics Manager

Objective
To develop one-two combinations and player movement (timing) at high speed with a third man run.

Description
In this variation, the sequence is basically the same as the previous practice, but we now add a diagonal pass and a third man run.

Player A passes to Player B, moves forward to receive the pass back and passes across to Player C. At the same time, Player B times his movement around the cone to receive the next pass from Player C and plays the ball out in front of C to run onto.

To finish the sequence, Player C plays a 1-2 combination with Player D who dribbles the ball to the start position. Each player moves to the next position (A -> B -> C -> D) and the next player in line starts a new sequence. Run this exercise in both directions.

MOVING TO RECEIVE IN A ONE TOUCH PASSING DRILL

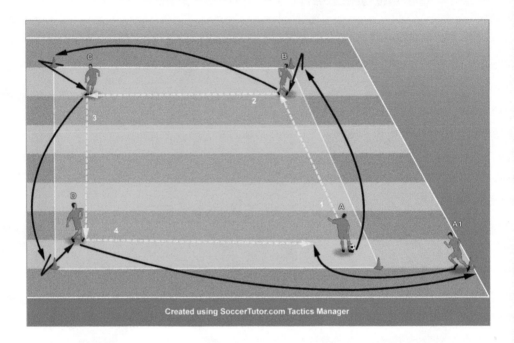

Objective
To develop checking away and timing the movement to receive in a 1 touch passing drill.

Description
In this practice, we have a group of 5 players in a 15 x 15 yard square. There is also an extra cone 5 yards to the side where A1 starts.

Player A passes to Player B, who checks away from the cone and passes to Player C who does the same. Player C then passes to D.

Player D completes the sequence by passing to position A and Player A1 times his movement from the cone at the side to repeat the same sequence again.

A moves to B, B to C, C to D, D to A1 and A1 to A (starting the sequence again).

Coaching Points
1. Players should have the correct body position when playing 1 touch passes - body half turned, allowing the ball to run across their body and pass with the back foot.
2. The timing of the movement is key to the rhythm of this drill.
3. Passes need to be correctly weighted and timed for each player to move onto and play a first time pass.
4. If a mistake is made, make sure to continue the same sequence.

'Y-SHAPE' - DRIBBLE, CHANGE DIRECTION + PASS

The Y shape is perhaps the most recurrent form of training in the history of football. The shape itself does not matter. However, what is important is that you meet the necessary match requirements through your practices.

When watching Louis van Gaal's training sessions, you feel you are in the right place to learn. He emphasises not only the technical implementation with all the details, but (especially in the run-up to the World Cup 2014) he emphasised the correct execution.

"Stay disciplined and focused, continue to demand more of yourself! Good progress."

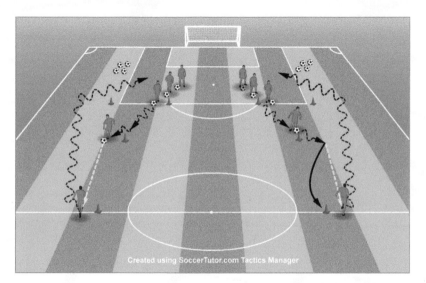

Description
Using half a full sized pitch, we divide the players into groups of between 5 and 8. We mark out the 'Y shapes' in the positions shown in the diagram. Player 1 dribbles to the cone, performs a feint/change of direction and passes to the player on the halfway line. The second player quickly dribbles the ball around the cone and to the start position. Each player moves to the next position and the next player at the start goes.

Variations
1. Have the players dribble the ball to the start position of the other group.
2. Either change the starting cone or have players starting from both sides.

Louis van Gaal's Instructions
• "Play the ball at the right pace."
• "Quick movement, fast rotation."
• "Quick dribble - only touch it three times to reach the starting point."
• "Passes should be flat, with no bounce along the ground."

PROGRESSION 'Y-SHAPE' - ONE-TWO COMBINATION, PASS + DRIBBLE

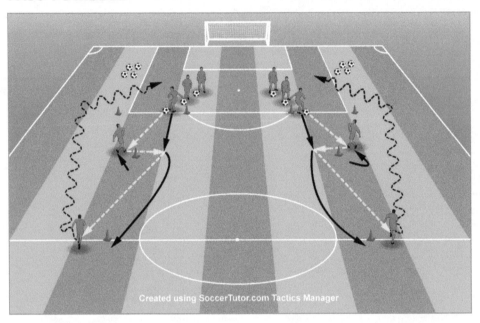

Created using SoccerTutor.com Tactics Manager

Description

In this progression of the previous practice, we now add a one-two combination at the second cone.

Player 1 plays a one-two combination with Player 2, moves forward to receive the pass back and passes to Player 3. The third player on the halfway line receives the pass and dribbles quickly around the cone to the start position.

Player 1 moves to Player 3's position and the next player goes. Rotate Player 2 often.

Variations

1. Have the players dribble the ball to the start position of the other group.
2. Either change the starting cone or have players starting from both sides.

PROGRESSION 'Y-SHAPE' - DOUBLE ONE-TWO COMBINATION, TIMING THE FORWARD RUN + DRIBBLE

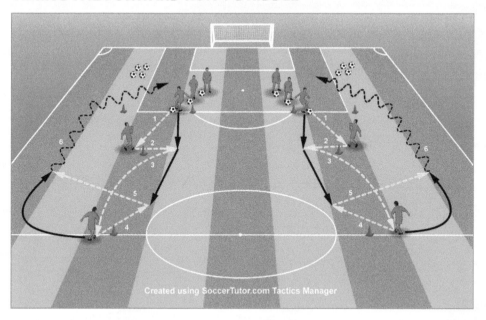

Description

In this second progression, we now have a double 1-2 combination in this 'Y shape' passing sequence. The first player plays a 1-2 combination with the second player, moves forward to receive the pass back and this time plays an aerial pass to the third player.

The player on the halfway line plays a first time cushioned volley pass back for the first player to run onto. The first player times his run and passes first time out wide for the third player to run onto and he finishes the sequence by dribbling quickly around the cone to the start position.

Player 1 moves to Player 3's position and the next player goes. Rotate Player 2 often.

Variation

1. Have the players dribble the ball to the start position of the other group.
2. Either change the starting cone or have players starting from both sides.

Progression

Add a passive defender for the final one-two combination to offer low resistance.

Coaching Points

1. For the aerial pass: "Put feeling in the pass, kick through the ball."

2. The timing and weight of pass is key for the one-two combinations in this drill.

5 v 3 AWARENESS TIME AND SPACE POSSESSION EXERCISE

In the last two years, we saw the Netherlands national team train in Katwijk, Kumarakom, various stadiums, during their training camp in Lagos (Portugal) and in Brazil during the World Cup.

Louis van Gaal: "To test the sense of awareness of new players within the Netherlands selection, and to improve this in all players, I often choose the 5v3 possession exercise."

The 5v3 possession exercise, according to Louis van Gaal, is well suited to judging the awareness of time and space. He used this exercise in the month building up to the World Cup to measure the potential of the players' awareness and positional play. Even during the World Cup, we saw this training exercise yet again.

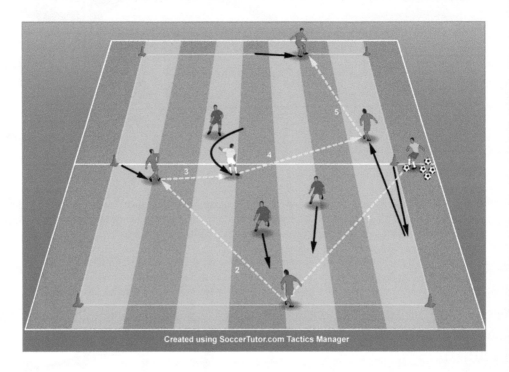

Created using SoccerTutor.com Tactics Manager

Objective
To develop positional play - passing, awareness of space and maintaining possession.

Description
In this 5v3 possession practice, we have 4 players positioned around the outside and 1 player in the middle (yellow). They aim to keep possession and the 3 blue defenders try to win the ball. The players should use the full width of the area.

The coach outside has plenty of balls and keeps playing a new ball in each time the 3 defenders win the ball or the ball goes out of play.

6 v 7 (+GK) ATTACK VS DEFENCE - COMBINATIONS TO BREAK THROUGH

Louis van Gaal: "Another drill we often choose is attack vs defence. For instance, we may train to tactically prepare the players for an opponent that is very defensive. We call it Plan B. We mainly coach the forwards on the solutions to disorganise such a defence."

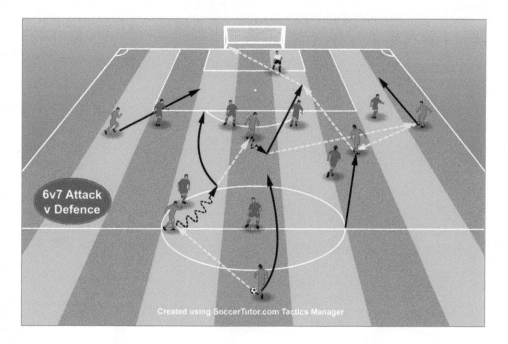

6v7 Attack v Defence

Created using SoccerTutor.com Tactics Manager

Objective
To develop attacking combinations and player movement to break through an organised defence.

Description
Using half a full sized pitch, we play attack vs defence. The attacking team aim to keep possession and then score in the goal with the goalkeeper. The defenders simply aim to prevent the attacking team from scoring by defending the goal.

This practice can be varied to practice in any formation you would like and can include more attackers/defenders depending on the numbers.

Coaching Points

1. The main aim is to use good movement to move the defenders out of their organised positions, which then creates space out wide or in behind to exploit.

2. Players should check away from their marker before moving to receive the ball.

3. The speed of play should be high so any gaps can be exploited before the defenders are able to recover or a teammate covers the space.

COLLECTIVE DEFENDING IN AN 8 v 7 GAME SITUATION

Louis van Gaal: "As a club coach I often preferred to use 8v7 practices with one big goal without a goalkeeper. You then have to feel when the time is right to apply pressure as a collective or instead defend the empty goal. This is a drill I loved to give as a club coach."

Created using SoccerTutor.com Tactics Manager

Objective
To develop the correct decision making as a collective defensive unit - when to drop and defend the goal and when to apply collective pressure.

Description
Using 2/3 of a full pitch we have 8 players defending a goal without a goalkeeper and 7 attacking players who start the practice in possession.

The orange attacking team aim to keep possession and use good passing combinations and movement to create a chance and score in the empty goal. The blue defenders must work collectively as a unit and defend the goal. If they win the ball, they can then counter attack and score a point if they dribble into the marked out zone as shown in the diagram.

Coaching Points
This practice is all about choosing the right time to apply pressure as a collective or instead defend the empty goal. We also work on passing combinations and player movement like in the previous practice.

POSITIONAL SUPPORT PLAY IN AN 8 (+2) v 8 (+2) POSSESSION GAME

The kind of training that we have seen from Van Gaal the most was the positional 8 (+2) v 8 (+2), which was in a slightly smaller space with a smaller numbers of players.

Louis van Gaal calls this a 'ball game'. Danny Blind and Patrick Kluivert stood diagonally opposite each other and played in the next ball to the teams. Van Gaal guarded the rules and whistled each time a new ball needed to be played in.

Because there are 2 players of each team on the outside, it is very suitable to give shape to the side. You can also rotate and rest certain players. When the entire squad was fit during the World Cup, 8 (+2) v 8 (+2) was used, as it was the day before the competitive matches. The three goalkeepers trained separately with Frank Hoek.

Objective
To develop positional play with a focus on possession - support movements and passing/receiving.

Description
In an area 25 x 35 yards, we play an 8 (+2) v 8 (+2) possession game. If you play a 7 (+2) v 7 (+2) game, then use a 25 x 30 yard area and if you play a 6 (+2) v 6 (+2) game, then use a 25 x 25 yard area.

In two opposite corners, the coaches alternate to pass a new ball to 'their' team each time the ball goes out of play.

This practice is all about the players providing support and creating the correct angles along with their teammates to maintain possession. The intensity should match that of a competitive match. You can limit the players to 2 touches to speed up play.

During training in the stadium the day before the World Cup matches, the Netherlands played this 8 (+2) v 8 (+2) possession game.

They performed five repetitions of 2 minutes with a rest of 1 minute after each repetition. They also swapped the role of the outside players after each repetition.

Coaching Points

1. In the last repetitions coach more aggressively, insisting your players defend/press collectively and then try to maintain possession of the ball directly after winning it, while always expressing the need for high focus.

2. The ball must never be still and must continually be moving, otherwise one of the coaches plays a new ball in to the other team.

Louis van Gaal's Instructions

- "Use all the space to keep possession."

- "Talk to each other, coach each other."

- "Move as a central player in the midfield line."

- "Make the space small when the other team have possession."

- "Never play the ball straight back to each other. After two short passes, play a long pass to follow."

- "This is a ball game. Use the full width. Find space where you can."

- "Keep the ball in your positions, you respect the distances to each other."

- "Move collectively. Together magnify, all together make the space small."

PASSING 'STATIONS' - CREATE SPACE, GIVE & GO + DRIBBLE IN A CONTINUOUS DRILL

Louis van Gaal often explains the players need to show more courage in possession and uses these passing 'stations' in his training sessions. This is to train the players to move through the lines (defence -> midfield -> attack).

The principle is to skip to the next 'station'. We first saw the Netherlands use this practice in May 2013 in Hoenderloo. The players were visibly well used to this drill and during the 2014 World Cup they performed it seamlessly.

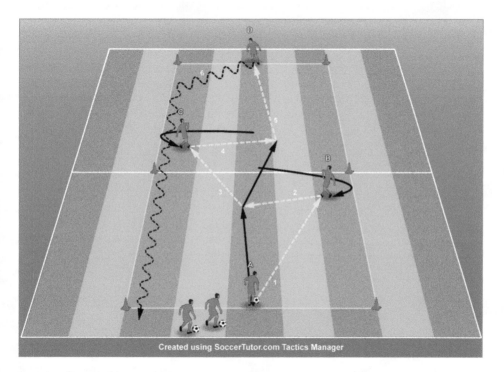

Created using SoccerTutor.com Tactics Manager

Objective
To develop combination play through the lines in the build-up play.

Description
In an area 10 x 30 yards (divided into two 10 x 15 yard zones), a minimum of 6 players participate in this passing combination practice.

There are a group of players (A) who start with a ball on one of the short sides. 2 players (B and C) start in the middle and Player D is positioned on the opposite short side. You can double occupy each position to speed up the exercise.

Player B checks away from the middle with a curved run and Player A plays a 1-2 combination with him, times the run forward and plays another 1-2 combination with Player C (who has also checked away with a curved run), moves forward again and makes his final pass to Player D.

Player D completes the sequence by dribbling the ball inside the lines back to the start position. Each player moves to the next position (A -> B -> C -> D) and the next player goes.

Coaching Point

This practice is to train players to make combinations to move through from the defensive line, through the midfield line and finally into the final third.

VARIATION PASSING 'STATIONS' - CREATE SPACE, THIRD MAN RUN + DRIBBLE IN A CONTINUOUS DRILL

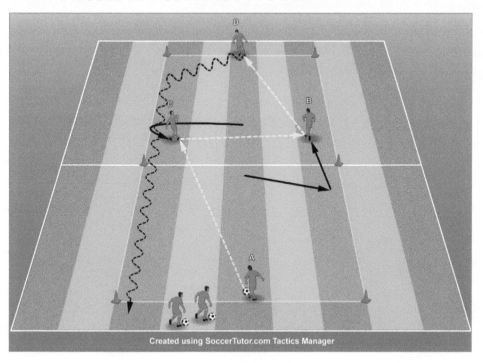

Created using SoccerTutor.com Tactics Manager

Description

In this variation, we remove the first one-two combination and add a third man run.

Players B and C both check away from the middle, but this time Player A passes to Player C. Player C then plays a first time pass to Player B who has made a second movement forward.

To complete the sequence Player B passes to Player D who dribbles the ball inside the lines back to the start position. Each player moves to the next position (A -> B -> C -> D) and the next player goes.

Progression

Add a passive defender between Players B and C to replicate a real match situation.

PROGRESSION **PASSING 'STATIONS' - CREATE SPACE, GIVE & GO, THIRD MAN RUN + DRIBBLE IN A CONTINUOUS DRILL**

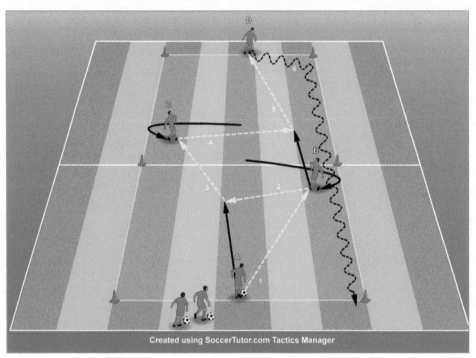

Created using SoccerTutor.com Tactics Manager

Description

In this progression, we play the first one-two combination and a third man run follows.

Player B checks away from the middle with a curved run and Player A plays a 1-2 combination with him, times the run forward and passes to Player C (who has also checked away with a curved run). At the same time, Player B makes a third man run to move forward, receive the next pass from C and pass to Player D.

Player D completes the sequence by dribbling the ball inside the lines back to the start position. Each player moves to the next position (A -> B -> C -> D) and the next player goes.

Progression

Add a goal and a goalkeeper so that when Player B passes to Player D, he lays it off for him to shoot on goal.

VARIATION PASSING 'STATIONS' - CREATE SPACE, GIVE & GO, THIRD MAN RUN + DRIBBLE IN A CONTINUOUS DRILL (2)

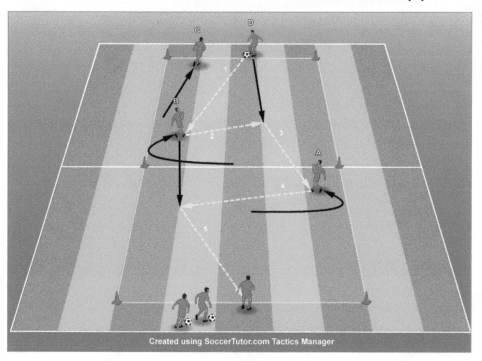

Variation

This variation to the previous practice has one simple change. Player D does not dribble the ball back to the start position and player C moves into his position.

Once the ball reaches Player D, he then starts the same combination back in the opposite direction towards the start position. This is fully displayed in the diagram.

Player C has moved into D's position, D moves to where B is, B moves to where A is and A moves to the start position. The next player goes.

HIGH SPEED OF PLAY QUICK FINISHING 6 v 6 SMALL SIDED GAME

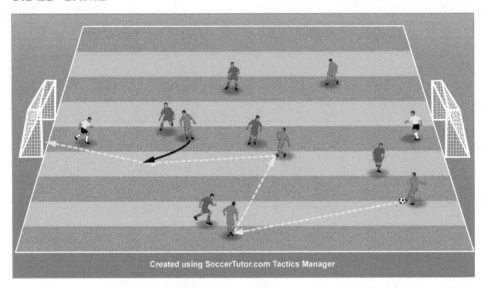

Created using SoccerTutor.com Tactics Manager

Objective
To develop quick play and finishing at every opportunity.

Description
We perform 5 x 4 minute repetitions of this intensive small sided game, with 2 minutes recovery time after each repetition.

The important factor for this practice is to maintain a high intensity to replicate match conditions. Impose a 3 second rule for all set pieces and make sure the ball is constantly moving. If these rules are not met, transfer possession to the other team.

The goalkeepers are free to partake outfield to help maintain possession.

Louis van Gaal's Attacking Instructions
- "With conviction shoot. Shoot quickly."
- "When you take risks, you get the rewards."
- "Even if you are tired, keep doing what you do."
- "Have one player at the point of the attack, as a target man."
- "When everything is fixed, then shoot yourself in the other goal." (Keeper)

Louis van Gaal's Defensive Instructions
- "Cover on the inside."
- "Inside closed, force them to the outside."

POSITIONAL PLAY IN A 7 v 3 POSSESSION GAME

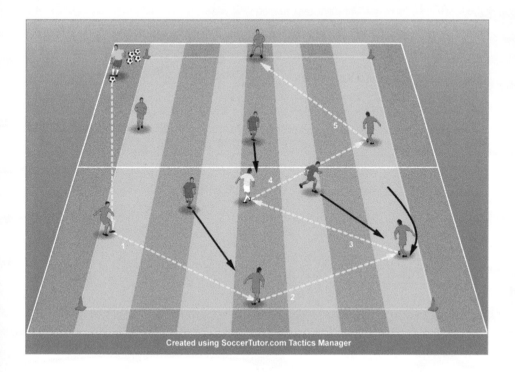

Created using SoccerTutor.com Tactics Manager

Objective
To develop positional play - passing, awareness of space and maintaining possession.

Description
In this 7v3 possession practice, we have 6 players who are positioned around the outside and 1 player in the middle (yellow). They aim to keep possession and the 3 blue defenders try to win the ball. The players are limited to 2 touches and should use the full width.

The coach outside has plenty of balls and keeps playing a new ball in each time the 3 defenders win the ball or the ball goes out of play.

Make it a competition and keep score. The team in possession get a point for a certain number of consecutive passes and the defenders win a point if they win the ball or the ball goes out of play.

Louis van Gaal's Instructions
- "Try to open up so you can see all the available space."
- "Put pressure on when the pass is sloppy or when the ball is in the corner."
- "Defenders, coach each other and apply joint pressure."

ATTACK FORMATION (2-3-2) v DEFENCE CROSSING AND FINISHING PRACTICE

We saw the attacking formations of 2-3-2 and 4-2 in November 2012, but there was still no 5-3-2 or a derivative thereof as we have frequently seen during the World Cup. However, we did see the Netherlands practice here for the scenario of a second striker.

We saw Dirk Kuyt and Leroy Fer in centre midfield for this exercise. It was striking that in this variation, the left-footed Robben was on the right and the right footed Lens played on the left, so in-swinging crosses were mainly used.

Objective
To practice attacking combinations, in-swinging crosses and finishing within a 2-3-2 attacking formation.

Description
Using half a full sized pitch, we have a 7 v 6 (+GK) attack v defence practice. The attacking team are in a 2-3-2 formation and the defending team are in a 4-2 formation.

The ball starts with the coach on the halfway line who passes to a member of the attacking team to start. The attacking team try to score in the goal past the goalkeeper. The defending team try to defend their goal and win the ball.

As we are using two strikers we practice this scenario realistically, with the strikers working together to create space and make different runs into the box - one to the near post and one to the far post.

Louis van Gaal's Instructions
- "High ball tempo. Defensive organisation."
- "Wing Forwards: Play as wide as you can!"
- "Use the switch when you can pass to a winger in space."
- "After losing possession, pressure the ball."
- "Try to get our two strikers. Until a cross."

VARIATION PRESS HIGH UP THE PITCH, WIN THE BALL AND COUNTER ATTACK IN A 7 v 6 (+GK) PRACTICE

Description

In this variation to the precious practice, add an extra full sized goal on the halfway line and start the practice with the blue team's goalkeeper.

The orange team then try to press high, win the ball and score.

SWITCH OF PLAY, 1 v 1 FLANK PLAY + CROSSING AND FINISHING PRACTICE

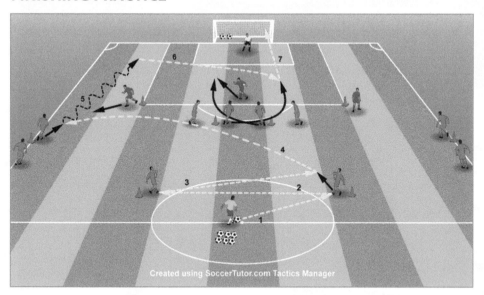

Created using SoccerTutor.com Tactics Manager

Description
Using half a full sized pitch, we mark out 8 cones as shown. We have 2 central midfield players near the halfway line, wingers/wide midfielders near the touchline and forwards near the edge of the penalty area. We also have 3 passive defenders (blue).

Use the players in their correct positions. The coach starts with the ball and passes to a centre midfielder who combines with the other one before a switch of play to the flank.

The wide player must receive the ball and is faced with a passive defender. They must react depending on the pass received and the positioning of their opponent and their teammates. In the diagram example, he beats the defender and crosses from the byline.

The 2 forwards must time their runs into the box (opposed by 1 passive defender), preferably with one going to the near post and the other to the far post.

Coaching Points
1. The coaches should build the resistance gradually, finishing with fully active defenders.

2. The exercise is easy to simplify working with fewer players and more repetitions.

3. Focus on the quality of execution for this practice.

Louis van Gaal's Instructions
- "Passing with purpose. An aerial ball straight to the man, or a tight pass along the ground, or a pass in front of him to move onto."
- "Timing! If you need to catch up as a striker then accelerate. Do not go too early, do not be late and work with each other."

SWITCHING PLAY IN A BOX FORMATION 5 v 5 SMALL SIDED GAME WITH OUTFIELD GOALKEEPERS

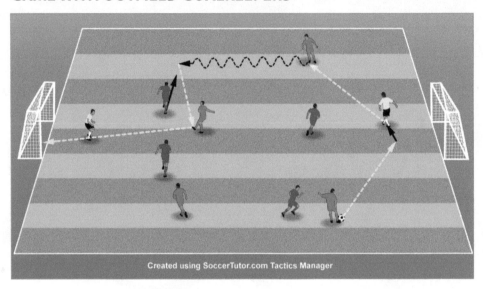

Created using SoccerTutor.com Tactics Manager

Objective
Developing quick switches of play and finishing in a small sided game.

Description
We perform 5 x 5 minute repetitions of this intensive small sided game, with 2 minutes recovery time after each repetition.

The teams should be in a box formation and look to keep possession and switch play before shooting at goal. Impose a 3 second rule for all set pieces and make sure the ball is constantly moving. If these rules are not met, transfer possession to the other team.

The goalkeepers are free to partake outfield to help maintain possession.

Louis van Gaal's Attacking Instructions
• "Use the keeper as a free man."
• "Open up as quickly as possible on the other side."
Louis van Gaal's Defensive Instructions
• "Cover on the inside."
• "Hold the opponent up under complete pressure."

SHOOTING PRACTICE WITH ONE-TWO COMBINATIONS (1)

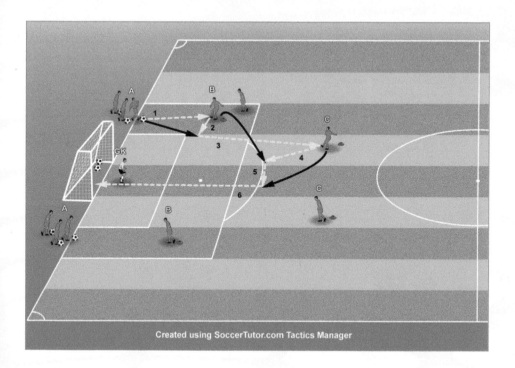

Created using SoccerTutor.com Tactics Manager

Objective

To develop quick combination play and shooting from the edge of the penalty area.

Description

We position the players on cones in the positions shown with 3 stations on each side of the penalty area.

Player A plays a 1-2 combination with Player B (cushioned pass) and then passes to Player C. Player B then makes a run to the edge of the box where Player C takes a touch and passes to him. Player B passes out in front of Player C to the edge of the penalty area.

The sequence is completed when Player C shoots at goal. Player A moves to B, B to C and C to the back of the line on the other side. The same sequence is then repeated from the opposite side of the penalty area.

Coaching Points

1. The accuracy and weight of the passes needs to be correct.

2. Timing of runs and angle of approach is very important for fluid play.

3. Monitor the shooting technique and be alert for rebounds.

CHAPTER 5

Louis van Gaal Training Practices from AZ Alkmaar, Bayern Munich & Manchester Utd

AZ ALKMAAR COACHING POSITIONAL ROLES TO BUILD UP PLAY IN A 6 ZONE 8 v 8 (+GK) FUNCTIONAL PRACTICE

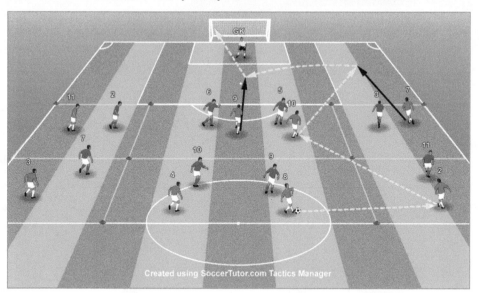

Created using SoccerTutor.com Tactics Manager

Objective
This practice enables players to learn how to operate in their specific positional zones in relation to their teammates and direct opponents. This is perfect to coach building up play.

Description
For this practice we play 8v8 (+GK) in half a full sized pitch. The area in between the halfway line and the edge of the box is split into 6 zones as shown. The red team try to build up play and score in the goal and the blues defend the goal and try to win the ball.

Each zone contains players in specific positions. Each side zone has 1 full back and 1 wide midfielder. Each central zone has 2 forwards and 2 centre backs (or midfielders). The players cannot leave their zones unless the ball is played behind (as shown in the diagram).

Progression
Add 2 mini goals 5 or 10 yards beyond the halfway line so if the defenders win the ball, they have the objective to counter attack and score.

Coaching Points
1. You should adapt this practice to specific game situations (and change the formation) for your team and focus on specific aspects for each phase.

2. If there is something your team does well or badly in their build up play or defensive organisation, you can use this exercise to demonstrate.

PROGRESSION COACHING POSITIONAL ROLES TO BUILD UP PLAY IN A 7 ZONE 11 v 11 GAME

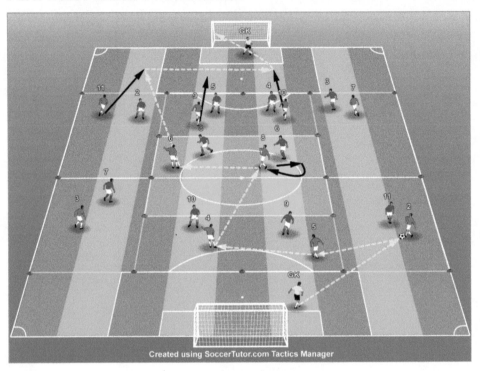

Created using SoccerTutor.com Tactics Manager

Objective

The objective is different to the previous practice as both teams look to score. If a defending team wins the ball, they can then attack (quick transition for both teams).

Description

For this practice, we play 11v11 on a full sized pitch. The area in between the 2 penalty boxes is divided into 7 zones as shown. The ball starts with the goalkeeper and the teams build up play and both teams try to keep possession and score.

Each zone contains players in specific positions. Each side zone has 1 full back and 1 wide midfielder, the 2 smaller central zones each have 2 centre backs and 2 forwards and the large central zone is where the 4 central midfield players play. The players are not allowed to leave their zones unless the ball is played in behind (as shown in the diagram).

Coaching Point

Within the large central zone, the players need to show good movement to create space, receive and move the ball into other zones or in behind the defensive line.

BAYERN MUNICH TIMING OF MOVEMENT IN DOUBLE ONE-TWO TRIANGLE PASSING COMBINATION

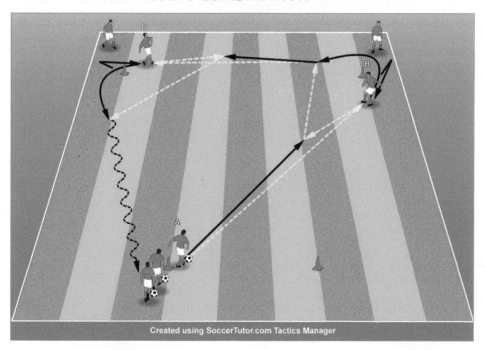

Created using SoccerTutor.com Tactics Manager

Objective
Improves short/medium range passing and timing of movement - quick combination play.

Description
We have players positioned on 3 cones 10-15 yards apart (minimum 2 on each). Player A passes diagonally to Player B who checks away and plays a cushioned pass back for A to run onto. Player A passes back to B again for him to run around the cone onto.

Player B then passes to C who checks away and plays a cushioned pass back. The final pass is by Player B in front of Player C to run round the cone onto and dribble back to the start position. Player A moves to B, B to C and the next player starts the same sequence again.

Variation
Start from the empty cone so that the players practice passing from different angles.

Coaching Points
1. Players should be moving when meeting the ball to increase the speed of play.
2. Open body shape - half turned and receive/pass with the back foot.
3. Runs/movements when creating space should be done at pace.

PROGRESSION TIMING OF MOVEMENT IN DOUBLE ONE-TWO PASSING COMBINATION + DRIBBLE

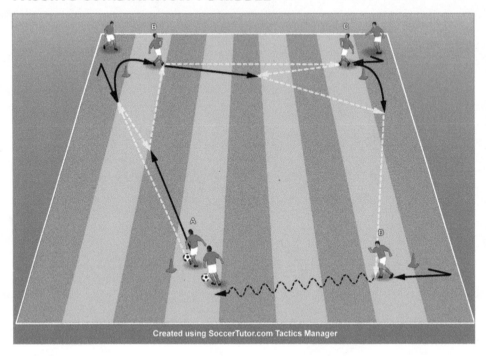

Created using SoccerTutor.com Tactics Manager

Description
In this progression to the previous practice, we move the fourth cone a little as shown and position a player there.

Player A passes to B who checks away and plays a cushioned pass back for A to run onto. Player A then passes back to B again for him to run around the cone onto.

Player B then passes to C who checks away and plays a cushioned pass back. Player B then passes the ball in front of Player C to run around the cone onto and pass to D. Player D checks away, receives and dribbles back to the start position.

Player A moves to B, B to C, C to D and the next player starts the same sequence again.

Coaching Points
1. Players should move to meet the ball to increase the speed of play.
2. Open body shape - half turned and receive/pass with the back foot.
3. Runs/movements when creating space should be done at pace.

MANCHESTER UNITED
PASSING DIAMOND WITH QUICK COMBINATION PLAY

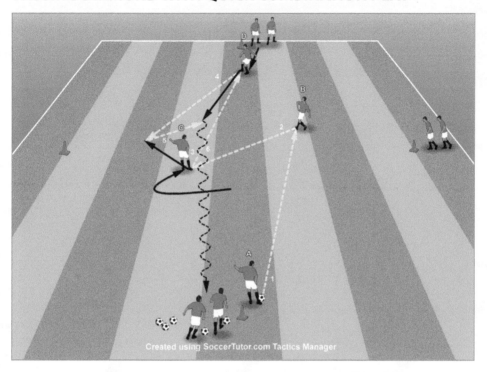

Objective
To develop passing, receiving and quick combination play.

Description
In a 20 x 15 yard area, we have 4 players involved in the combination with extra players behind 3 cones, leaving one empty. Player A passes to Player B and at the same time Player C opens up and moves to receive the next pass and pass to Player D.

Player C then opens up from inside to out and Player D plays a 1-2 combination with him. This quick 1-2 combination completes the sequence as Player D receives the ball back and dribbles to the start position.

A moves to B, B to C, C to D and D moves to A (dribbles the ball).

Coaching Points
1. Use a half-turn body shape and the back foot to pass and receive.

2. The timing and weight of pass is key, making sure the ball is played ahead of the next player to run onto.

VARIATION

PASSING DIAMOND WITH QUICK COMBINATION PLAY (2)

Description
In this variation to the previous practice, after C passes to D, Player D then plays a 1-2 combination with Player B instead of Player C (as shown in the diagram) and dribbles the ball back to the start position.

A moves to B, B to C, C to D and D moves to A (dribbles the ball).

MANCHESTER UNITED
SHOOTING PRACTICE WITH ONE-TWO COMBINATIONS (2)

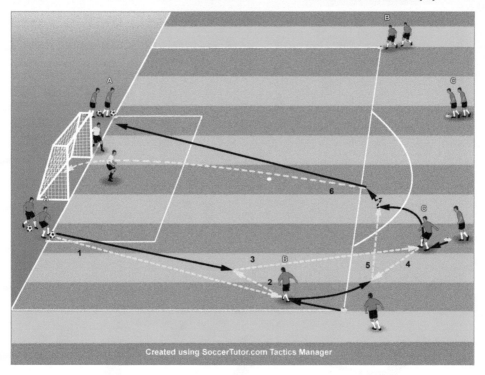

Created using SoccerTutor.com Tactics Manager

Objective
To develop quick combination play and shooting from the edge of the penalty area.

Description
We position the players on cones in the positions shown with 3 stations on each side of the penalty area.

Player A plays a 1-2 combination with Player B (cushioned pass) and then passes to Player C. Player B then makes a backwards movement where Player C passes to him. Player B passes out in front of Player C to the edge of the penalty area.

The sequence is completed when Player C shoots at goal. Player A moves to B, B to C and C to the back of the line on the other side. The goalkeepers switch and the same sequence is repeated on the opposite side of the penalty area.

Coaching Points
1. The accuracy and weight of the passes needs to be correct.
2. Timing of runs and angle of approach is very important for fluid play.
3. Monitor the shooting technique and be alert for rebounds.

MANCHESTER UNITED
SET PLAY: SHORT CORNER - CROSS AND FINISH

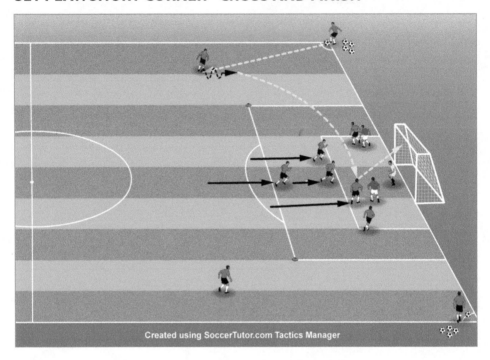

Created using SoccerTutor.com Tactics Manager

Objective
To practice short corner set play, crossing and finishing.

Description
In this practice we have 2 players in each corner and 1 attacker + 1 defender positioned in front of each post. There are a further 4 players who start outside the penalty area; 3 players positioned on the edge of the box and 1 deeper behind them.

The first player passes back to the second player who takes a touch and delivers a cross into the box. The 4 players positioned near the posts must react quickly and try to defend/attack the cross respectively.

The other 4 attacking players time their runs into the box and try to score. If the goalkeeper saves an attempt on goal or a defender clears the ball, keep playing (attempting to score) until the ball is dead. Then continue from the opposite corner.

Coaching Points
1. Focus on the runs of the attackers, making sure they all attack different areas and time their runs into the box well.

2. The defenders must react quickly and read the flight of the cross to clear the ball.

VARIATION
SET PLAY: IN-SWINGING CORNER AND FINISHING

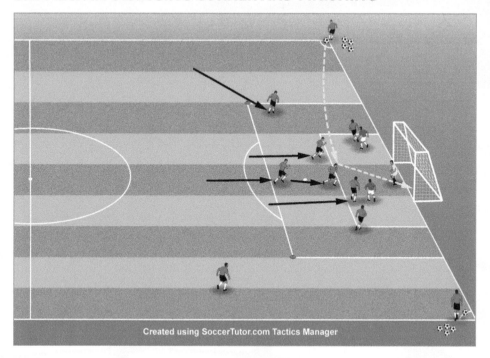

Created using SoccerTutor.com Tactics Manager

Objective
To practice in-swinging corner set play and finishing.

Description
In this variation from the previous we work with the same players. This time the player in the corner takes a conventional corner kick, crossing into the penalty area.

The player who crossed the ball in the previous practice now also makes a run into the box to help his team try to score a goal.

If the goalkeeper saves an attempt on goal or a defender clears the ball, keep playing (attempting to score) until the ball is dead. Then continue from the opposite corner.

MANCHESTER UNITED
SET PLAY: WIDE FREE-KICK - TIMING OF RUNS AND FINISHING

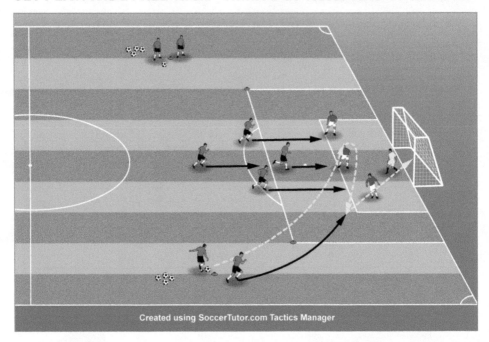

Created using SoccerTutor.com Tactics Manager

Objective

To practice attacking wide free kicks, timing of runs and finishing.

Description

In this practice we have 2 players near each sideline by a cone. There are 3 defenders in the box positioned as shown and there are 4 more attacking players who start outside the penalty area; 3 players positioned on the edge of the box and 1 deeper behind them.

The first player delivers a cross into the box. The 4 attacking players time their runs into the box and try to score. The player next to the player who crosses the ball also makes a run into the box to react to any defensive clearances.

If the goalkeeper saves an attempt on goal or a defender clears the ball, keep playing (attempting to score) until the ball is dead. Then continue from the opposite corner.

Variation

Instead of crossing directly from the free kick, the player can pass along the sideline for his teammate to cross and then make a run into the box himself.

CHAPTER

6

Data Analysis and the Periodization of Fitness Training

Text: Paul Geerars

Data Analysis and the Periodization of Fitness Training

The 2009-2010 season will live on as the period where Louis van Gaal, much sooner than expected, brought Bayern München back to the top level of European football. As a professional publication we felt obligated to describe the details of his approach which were so successful, which haven't been discussed so far. We ended up with an advanced technological system, LPM Soccer 3D, which Van Gaal deploys to set up his football conditioning objectives and tactical analysis. The full explanation thereby, of course after permission of Van Gaal himself, was given by the Dutch exercise physiologist Jos van Dijk.

Jos van Dijk
Exercise physiologist at Bayern München

His tasks include the planning and periodization of the football conditioning training for FC Bayern München's first team. Furthermore, he's also involved in monitoring and assessing the fitness of the team and individual players.

In collaboration with the fitness coaches, Jos van Dijk customises individual training programmes for the players and analyses data derived from training sessions and official matches. Jos van Dijk studied kinesiology (process of body movement), owns the diploma Trainer-Coach-1 and is a lecturer at the KNVB. Before he started working for FC Bayern München, he had a similar position at Willem II and AZ.

GERMANY: FC BAYERN MÜNCHEN

While being proclaimed the best coach of the year in the Netherlands the year before joining Bayern München, Van Gaal has now received a similar type of recognition in Germany. He won the coach of the year award in the Bundesliga, won the championship, the national cup (DFP-Pokal), reached the Champions League final and the style of play undoubtedly played a big part! Van Gaal likes to leave nothing to chance as a coach. One of his conditions to start working at FC Bayern München was that they install an advanced technological system, which he already had good experiences with at AZ. This was done in collaboration with Max Reckers, now also employed by Bayern. With the help of the system (LPM Soccer 3D) an extreme amount of data can be measured during training, such as heart rate, distance covered, positioning, speed and accelerations/sprints of each player. Basically dozens of times per second the mounted 'beacons' around the training ground register the position of each player who is wearing a bib with sensors. In contrast to a GPS guided system, there is a very high measuring accuracy. This is important because small accelerations or

changes in direction can have a big impact within football.

From the very first training session at Bayern this technology had to be in effect. Prior to that first training session, all players immediately received a specially prepared bib. Van Gaal set the tone immediately by walking up to everyone to check whether the bib was worn. For Jos van Dijk, exercise physiologist at Bayern, this meant he was able to do an outstanding job from the beginning given the perfect conditions.

FOOTBALL CONDITIONING

Jos van Dijk: "The performance of the players and the team is dependant on many factors. One of these factors is football conditioning. For instance, we know that players make around 20-40 sprints in matches, accelerate every 30 seconds on average, run 4-12 km in a match, engage in 40-60 duels and play the game at 85-90% of their maximum heart rate. They have to be capable of carrying out their football actions to their best quality for 90 minutes. But the most important thing is that the players keep making the right decisions, even if they are fatigued. Excellent football conditioning

has to support all of this. If we look at football actions in key moments, then these can be linked to various components of football conditioning. We distinguish, amongst others, speed over the first few metres, starting speed, the ability to accelerate, duel strength, jumping strength, aerobic ability and the capacity to keep making movements for 90 minutes. It's clear that the requirements that are being set in the match can differ for each position. They also relate closely to the chosen style of play. (see figure 1).

Figure 1. Olympique Lyon Vs FC Bayern München - Distance Covered in First Half.
Hi-run: Number of High Intensity Runs at Speed of 21-24 Km/hour.

Player Position	Sprints (m)	Hi-Runs (m)	Total (m)
Goalkeeper	0	9	3221
Full backs	154	107	5625
Centre backs	34	100	5511
Centre midfielders	28	172	5964
Wide midfielders	252	235	6014
Number 10	486	231	6167
Number 9	286	182	6281
Average	171	164	5867

Louis van Gaal acknowledges that football conditioning is one of the key performance indicators in top football. That's why he dedicates a lot of training time to the development and maintenance of the football conditioning, especially in football specific drills. Therefore we look at what's required on a team level, but they also spend a lot of time on the individual positions. In football specific conditioning drills, players always train within their own position and get addressed not only on the requirements for that position, but also

conditioning wise. We plan individual training a few times a week, whereby the players follow their own programme."

FITNESS ANALYSIS

The technology can work as good as you like, but it's crucial that the head coach clearly explains what type of information he's mainly interested in. Thanks to the previous experiences at AZ this wasn't a problem for Louis van Gaal.

Jos van Dijk: "At AZ the technical staff worked with LPM Soccer 3D and we had good experiences with it. Louis van Gaal announced that he wants to have this measuring system at his disposal at FC Bayern München as well. The top German club stands for innovation and always searches for opportunities, which new technologies have to offer, in order to gain a competitive advantage. Thus, the system fit the demands very well.

We use the measuring system LPM Soccer 3D every day to monitor the training load of the players from Bayern. The players wear a bib where measuring sensors have been affixed. The data which this generates is used to find out whether the players accomplish the set physical training objectives and how the fitness level of the players develops. We also utilise the measurement data for a better periodization of the intensity and extent of the training load within a week, and over weeks. We avoid under working or overloading during training. This applies on a team level, as well as on an individual level. This pays off with a fitter team, better performances and less injuries. Our training sessions are monitored on a daily level and the information this generates is being used for individual feedback and the

85

Figure 2. Capacity and Maximum Speed over 28 Repetitions of 15 Metres

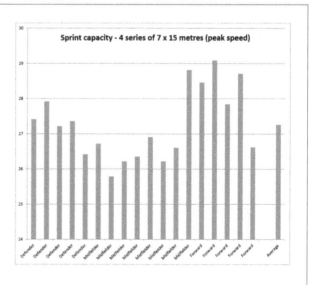

Position of Player	Average Peak Speed
Defender	27.41
Defender	27.92
Defender	27.22
Defender	27.36
Defender	26.41
Midfielder	26.72
Midfielder	25.79
Midfielder	26.22
Midfielder	26.35
Midfielder	26.91
Midfielder	26.22
Midfielder	26.6
Midfielder	28.82
Forward	28.46
Forward	29.09
Forward	27.84
Forward	28.71
Forward	26.62
Average	27.26

planning of the next training sessions. The main advantage of LPM Soccer 3D is that it provides an extremely accurate measure of the players' positions on the pitch. It illustrates the following; each player's physical output, ability (speed, accelerations) as well as capacity (distances in different zones of speed and accelerations). By linking this to other data, such as the assessment of the implementation by the coach, course of the heart rate, and also the players' own assessment, we get a detailed overview of the complete programme of football conditioning. For clarification, I will elaborate on a concrete example from practice at Bayern München. We've trained the sprint capacity based on 4 series of 7 x 15 metres. The results were illustrated with two figures by LPM Soccer 3D (figure 2 above and figure 3 on the next page).

Figure 2 and *3* provide an insight into some of the system's abilities. Figure 2 shows the capacity and the maximum speed the players generate over 28 repetitions of 15 metres. It's clearly visible that the forwards score higher than the midfielders, while the defenders are between the two in terms of capacity. On an individual scale the differences are big.

Figure 3 (next page) shows the data of three players; a defender, a midfielder and a forward. The defender has an average score regarding the football conditioning factor, but in the fourth series he's no longer capable of delivering the same capacity. The decline is higher than 7% and this means that he can improve his reach. In addition, the scores of the midfielder, who clearly has less capacity in speed, experiences no difficulties when carrying out the 4 series. The number of repetitions (size of the capacity training) could be expanded. Training of the capacity and speed might also be valuable for this player.

The third player in this exercise, a forward,

reaches the highest average maximum speed of the three players. He's also capable to perform at full capacity in the fourth series. He's still able to make his moves in the last 20 minutes of the game and be decisive. In this way we can extract valuable information from the training data about the players, content and dosage of the training."

Figure 3. Football Conditioning Data of a Defender, a Midfielder and a Forward

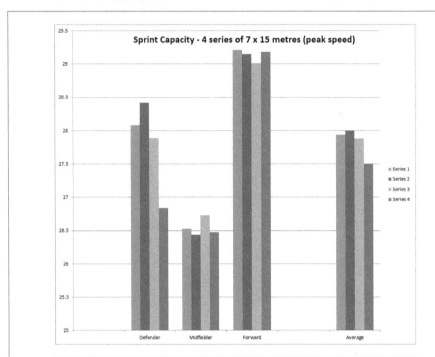

Peak Speed	Series 1	Series 2	Series 3	Series 4
Defender	28.08	28.42	27.89	26.84
Midfielder	26.53	26.44	26.73	26.48
Forward	29.21	29.15	29.01	29.18
Average	27.94	28.00	27.88	27.50

INTERPRETING DATA

Jos van Dijk: "Basically, during the football conditioning drills, the LPM Soccer 3D system is used to measure. This way we're provided with a view of not only the training load based on the heart rate, but also based on the football labour that's being carried out.

Figures 4 and *5* illustrate the data of a football conditioning training 6 v 6 with goalkeepers.

Figure 4 and 5. Metres Covered Offset against the Heart Rate in a Football Conditioning Drill (7 v 7 Small Sided Game)

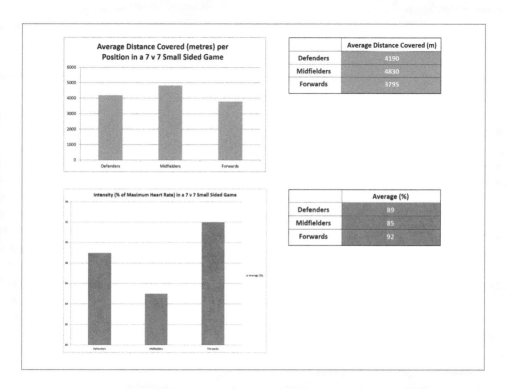

We offset the metres covered in this training session (figure 4) against the training intensity, based on the heart rate (figure 5). If we only look at the heart rate, then the midfielder experiences the least load (85%), the defender is in the middle (89%), whilst the forward experiences the most strenuous load (92%) during this training.

If we analyse the training load, in this case the metres covered, then the picture is entirely different. Now we can see that the midfielder has put in the most work, followed by the defender and in last place, the forward. We can conclude from this that the midfielder has good conditioning. He's capable of carrying out a large training load at a relatively low heart rate. The forward can thus improve himself regarding this aspect of his conditioning.

Match data has to make it clear to what extent this is a restricting factor for him in relation to the execution of his tasks and making moves on the pitch. In this way, we've set up a football conditioning profile for every player. We benchmark this against the profile for that position. The position within the style of play is decisive for the labour a player has to deliver and the corresponding intensity. This produces the profile that belongs to a position in our style of play."

Figure 6. Olympique Lyon (Blue) Vs Fc Bayern München (Red) - Player Positioning and Distances between Players and Lines in the Game

Chris (Lyon) has the ball and is building up play.

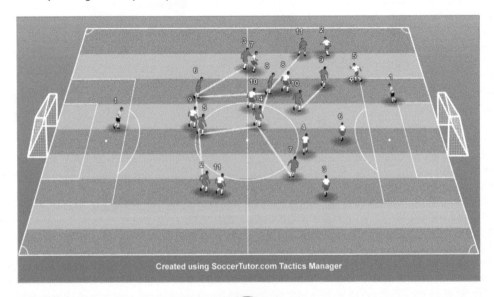

Created using SoccerTutor.com Tactics Manager

TACTICAL ANALYSIS

Jos van Dijk: "The LPM Soccer 3D software also provides the possibility to perform tactical analysis. The foundation for this is a precise determination of the players' position and the ball at any moment in the game. That's how we get a dynamic picture, especially in size and numbers, of aspects which relate to our style of play during the key moments. This provides many areas of application. One of these possibilities is the assessment of the player positioning in a defensive organisation. We use animations where the mutual distances between the central defenders (Daniel Van Buyten and Martin Demichelis/Holger Badstuber) and the two defensive midfielders (Bastian Schweinsteiger and Mark van Bommel) when the opposition are in possession plays a key role in relation to the ball and the opposition *(figure 6)*. This has an impact on our defensive organisation, the spaces we give away to the opposition and the ability to defend forwards with these players. For the coaching and the discussion of situations with the players, this is an excellent tool.

Another application is the transition from attack to defence when we lose the ball and the role our forwards play in this phase. The visuals of the training sessions and matches are being used to make the execution of tasks and functions visible for the players. What do the players have to do when they lose the ball, and what do they do in reality? It can be very enlightening to show this to the players with the help of footage. This of course is very useful in terms of coaching the players to perfect the execution of our preferred style of play. During the possession phase for instance, we look at the space in the attacking sense for the forwards and the possibilities to play between the lines.

The player positioning in front of the goal on the flanks, as well as early or late crosses

are also a topic of discussion. There is always progress to be made in this area. The technical staff discusses such issues with our players.

During these discussions, the key game moments are played back and analysed. The central focus here is the collaboration between several players in one line, but also between the lines - attack, midfield and defence. This subsequently translates to targeted training labour.

Max Reckers is a specialist and plays his own role within this process. He knows the technological systems and their possibilities inside out and is intensively involved with technological innovations. He's responsible for coding our matches to the key moments in football actions and he takes care of the technical support when preparing the pre-match or post-match discussion. This happens on a team level, but also with players individually and line discussions by Louis van Gaal."

3D GAME ANALYSIS

Louis van Gaal doesn't have much use for 2D-visuals of, for example formations, but he prefers placing his players 'in the situation' (3D), to clarify matters to them. On the pitch, or virtually.

Jos van Dijk: "The 3D option within LPM Soccer 3D offers the ability to look at football situations throughout the position of the player. Game situations can be played back again and together with the player, then can be checked which options were possible. With our left back for instance, we've comprehensively talked about which options he has during ball possession. This

usually happens on the pitch with a flat tactical board which every football coach has. Thanks to the new 3D technology we can play back the situations from the game or training and bring that player back into that specific situation. Within the dynamic of the game or training situation, time and space, the correct or wrong decisions which a player makes can then be discussed. If necessary, other players get involved as well, because they have to be available for a pass at the right moment. This provides many insights to players who have to solve football situations collectively. Thus, the 3D application basically shows the additional possibilities for coaching the players.

For matches we use a different type of technology to determine, amongst others, the position data of players and opponents. This information however, can also be processed and analysed by the LPM Soccer 3D software. By now we have an accurate picture of the demands that the games require from our players. In the area of conditioning we distinguish between levels (Bundesliga/Champions League) and the position of a player. We use this to dose the training load and the nature of the conditioning training e.g. in certain phases of the season we want to give a conditioning overload in training compared to the game load."

Bayern München was very hot and experienced a fantastic season. That's the great merit of Louis van Gaal, who's proving again to be one of the best coaches in the world. One key element of a top coach is that he leaves nothing to chance and takes every detail into account which can be of any influence to the success of his team. Therefore, Van Gaal also used LPM Soccer 3D at Bayern, the system which partially explains why his players are still in excellent shape during the final stages of the season.

LOCAL POSITION MEASUREMENT

LPM (Local Position Measurement) Soccer 3D is a tool to register all movements of the players during training. The (conditioning) coach is able to see every player at any time, where he is, what his speed is and how he makes his efforts.

The development of LPM Soccer 3D started in 2002 when the football club PSV and the TNO-department Industry and Technique collaborated to see if TNO could get more out of training seasons by using measurements. The people in charge back then were Guus Hiddink and exercise physiologist Luc van Agt.

The technology is installed on the training pitch at PSV in Eindhoven. It's managed by PSV, and supported by Frans Lefeber of Inmotio. The monitoring systems of Inmotio are based on a wireless communication system. LPM is a unique system that provides real-time measurements of positioning and heart activity. The real-time network is connected with several base stations, which are placed around the pitch that needs to be measured. The athletes wear a special bib with a transponder (transmitter) which sends the measured real-time performance data via antennas to the base stations.

Because of the high accuracy whereby the position of the athletes is determined (+/- 5 cm) and the high measuring frequency (up to 1000 times per second) the system generates extremely accurate information. The Inmotio system has an error percentage of < 1% (validation report of the Rijks Universiteit van Groningen). The position measurements are shown in 2D, as well as 3D with the help of the application software. The coach is able to look at various real-time data throughout every position on a tablet, and therefore is able to directly adjust the training of an individual athlete or of an entire team.

In addition to the measured real time performance data, the link with a time synchronised video system also generates the created video footage during the training sessions. With the monitoring system, the training of certain situations during training can also be easily evaluated with the player(s) afterwards.

CHAPTER SUMMARY

BAYERN MÜNCHEN

- The 2009-2010 season will live on as the period where Louis van Gaal, much sooner than expected, brought Bayern München back to the top level of European football.

- Louis van Gaal won the coach of the year award in the Bundesliga, won the championship, the national cup (DFP-Pokal), reached the Champions League final and introduced a very attractive and attacking style of play.

CONDITIONING

- Jon van Dijk (Exercise physiologist) tasks included the planning and periodization of the football conditioning training.

- A lot of training time was dedicated to the development and maintenance of the football conditioning, especially making sure to use football specific conditioning drills.

- Louis van Gaal and the fitness coaches also made sure to plan individual training a few times a week, where the players follow their own programme.

ANALYSIS OF PHYSICAL PERFORMANCE

- Jos van Dijk customises individual training programmes for the players and analyses data derived from training sessions and official matches.

- At Bayern, van Gaal used an advanced technological system, LPM Soccer 3D, deployed to achieve his football conditioning objectives and for tactical analysis.

- With the help of the system (LPM Soccer 3D) an extreme amount of data can be measured during training, such as heart rate, distance covered, positioning, speed and accelerations/sprints of each player.

- The information from the system showed players make around 20-40 sprints in matches, accelerate every 30 seconds on average, run 4-12 km in a match, engage in 40-60 duels and play the game at 85-90% of their maximum heart rate.

- **Jon van Dijk:** 'We distinguish, amongst others, speed over the first few metres, starting speed, the ability to accelerate, duel strength, jumping strength, aerobic ability and the capacity to keep making movements for 90 minutes. It's clear that the requirements that are being set in the match can differ for each position. They also relate closely to the chosen style of play.'

INTERPRETING DATA

- The measuring system LPM Soccer 3D was used every day to monitor the training load of Bayern's players. The players wear a bib with measuring sensors and the data which this generates is used to find out whether the players accomplish the set physical training objectives and how the fitness level of the players develops.

- The system is also utilised to determine the periodization of the intensity and extent of the training load within a week, and over weeks. This helps to avoid under working or overloading players during training sessions. The conclusion to this is a fitter team for all stages of the season, better performances and less injuries.

TACTICAL ANALYSIS

- With the technology available, van Gaal and his coaching staff could find out the players' positioning at any point of any game.

- This creates a dynamic picture of the team and enables the coaches to study the aspects which relate to the style of play during key moments of matches.

- For example, this information can be used to show the distances between each player when the opposition have possession of the ball, and if the distance was too much. This can then be discussed with players and coached during training.

CHAPTER

7

Coaching Players in the Situation and Creating a 'Winning Climate'

Text: Paul Geerars and Henny Kormelink

Coaching Players in the Situation and Creating a 'Winning Climate'

'Coaching players in the situation, that's what it's about'

According to then AZ head coach Louis van Gaal in 2006, the results of his team could only be assessed from November on. Therefore, De Voetbaltrainer spoke to the manager during that period. Van Gaal provides an insight into the way everything seems to fall into place this season at the club from Alkmaar, from the forwards to the kit man. 'There now is a top sport climate'.

Louis van Gaal is praised by many fellow coaches and players who have worked with him. His knowledge and expertise therefore are undisputed. However it's possible a coach with such outstanding qualities can still be dealing with a team that isn't functioning right and that was proven in the previous season. Apparently the figurative finger was put on the sore spot and appropriate measures were taken, because the following season AZ played attractive football and the results were very good.

The dramatic ending of the 2006/2007 season will continue to stay etched in people's minds for a while. AZ forfeited the league title in the very last game against Excelsior, an undesirable ending to a brilliant season. The objective for that season was to finish in the top 5, progress through a couple of rounds of the UEFA Cup and have a good performance in the national cup. Those expectations were far exceeded. Beforehand, all supporters of the club would have definitely taken a season where AZ competed for the league title up until the last minute, only to lose in the quarter finals of the UEFA Cup and at the same time reach the final of the national cup. However, the feeling afterwards was quite different and the media played a pivotal role. They mainly spoke of a failing AZ. In other words, during the season an ambition arises which surpasses that objective by far and eventually this translates to an enormous hangover. That growing ambition in Alkmaar ensured that the bar was raised at the start of last season. When the expectations aren't being met, the contrast is very big. Even a coach as experienced as Louis van Gaal visibly has difficulties with it. But now all pieces of the puzzle seem to fit once again at AZ. What's the main difference?

Louis van Gaal: "Also during last season we were the better team in 30 of the 34 matches. Then you should win at least 15 times, but that didn't happen. This then relates to your abilities to score. In addition, last year we were missing strong personalities due to long-lasting injuries. We were able to replace their football qualities, but not their personality. Martens, Schaars and Joey Didulica have a positive impact on the top sport climate in the locker room and on the pitch. They were missing at a time when they were needed the most, when we fell into a downward spiral."

Louis van Gaal attaches great value to 11 v 11 in training

STYLE OF PLAY
And the style of play has been changed…

Louis van Gaal: "At AZ we now play in a 4-4-1-1 formation, because in my opinion the team functions the best with this system. In Alkmaar I've originally started with the 4-3-3. But with Danny Koevermans, Moussa Dembélé and Shota Arveladze in the squad, I preferred to not put two of them on the bench. I thought that would be a shame and that's the reason I've chosen to play with two strikers. Positioning one of them as a winger wasn't an option for me either, because that position is only reserved for a specialist in my vision. The current choice at AZ isn't that surprising. As a coach you have to purely look at the qualities of a team at that given moment. During my early days at Ajax we also played in a 4-4-2 formation for a while. Because of the specific training and the possibilities on the transfer market at that time I was able to play with real wingers much more often.

At FC Barcelona I let the team play in three different ways in terms of the basic formation. Systems such as the 2-3-2-3 or the 3-2-3-2, depending on whether the opposition played with three or two forwards, don't really matter too much. All that matters is that it fits the players and the implementation of those players on the pitch. It's no problem to play in a 4-5-1 formation if you have a striker as a target man who can receive the ball with his back to goal very well. Stefan Petterson was like that at Ajax for instance. At AZ, Pellè is able to perform that role in an excellent way. He only has to score more, even though Petterson wasn't a top scorer either. He allowed others like Jari Litmanen and Dennis Bergkamp to score. But in reality it's not that important whether you play with one, two or three strikers. It's about the execution of the tasks and functions of all the different positions on the pitch. From every possible formation you'll end up playing in each zone of the pitch anyway. How do the players respond to each other? How do they play together? Are they organised and in tune as a team?"

PIECES OF THE PUZZLE

Louis van Gaal: "This season I've started the preparation of AZ with a style of play where Mounir El Hamdaoui enjoys great freedom. We basically created a position for him. Mounir has never scored as much as he did now. This doesn't surprise me at all. We see him as a 'second striker', next to Dembélé, Ari or Graziano Pellè. In addition, we have many players who are very versatile and who can play a supportive role in the midfield. We've also recruited other types of footballers. Jeremain Lens is a bit more individually orientated, while Nick van der Velden attempts to search for that

combination more often. Lens isn't as good as Martens in fulfilling the function of El Hamdaoui. His qualities lie elsewhere. You're in need of Lens when you want to play football a bit more forwards or if he has to deal with an opponent who he can take on. Simon Poulsen then again looks a bit more like Lens as a footballer, while Martens plays football in the combination more often."

'The pieces of the puzzle have to fall into place'

CREATIVITY

Louis van Gaal: "I want to have at least three creative players in my team. Currently we have a minimum of five at AZ. Martens is basically a creative player, but now has to play in the function of El Hamdaoui. He had to learn this. They are all pieces of a puzzle which have to fall into place. The process behind it requires time. I've already announced pre-season that you can only see where we stand with AZ from November onwards. Unfortunately Dembélé got injured, but Ari and Pellè are good replacements. Those two have played a whole season by now. They had to adjust to, for instance, the direct communication and thus also the type of coaching we apply in the Netherlands. As a football coach you have to take this background into account. Sometimes it's better to discuss criticism individually with the player in question. Thus, this requires more time and energy. Sometimes I make a different consideration and end up choosing to display my criticism in front of the entire group. This at first wasn't easy for them.

It's easily said, but we have to make sure that we score. On the other hand we have to try to avoid conceding goals. If we don't

'Unfortunately Dembélé got injured, but Ari and Pellè are good replacements.'

score, then pressure gets put on our defensive organisation. We don't want that. We don't exactly have a 'defensive team'. This means that our defenders are selected based on other qualities. Héctor Moreno and Niklas Moisander for instance, aren't top international defenders. Nevertheless they still perfectly fit to AZ. That's because we preach attacking football, where we wish to build-up from the back."

ELEVEN VERSUS ELEVEN

AZ lost the first 2 competitive matches of this season. This reminded many of the difficult previous season. Louis van Gaal was clear in his commentary however after the defeat against ADO Den Haag (3-0). He saw a good AZ side. The coach perceived a positive development, whereby only the goals were still absent. In the following

match the figurative turnaround happened. At home PSV were beaten by a score of 1-0. Afterwards, a long series of victories and only two draws followed.

Louis van Gaal: "During the preparation for the home game against PSV we trained behind closed doors three times - on Wednesday, Thursday and Friday. We then played 11 v 11 in three different formations. Those were training sessions where I could explain a lot to the players. PSV played in a set form at that time. Thus, we've mainly focused on our own game. Altering your formation isn't the only thing you can do as a coach. It's also about the interpretation which various players can apply to that same position. In addition, it's also about the balance in the team. For instance, at that time, Nick van der Velden, before the match against PSV, played very well in the

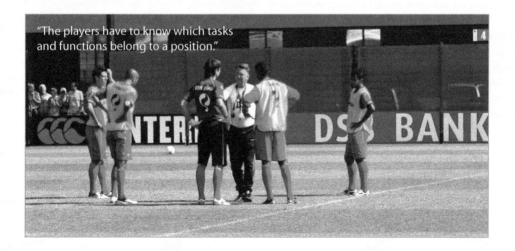

"The players have to know which tasks and functions belong to a position."

position of a false striker and for that reason he was also able to provide a lot of support to our midfield. In that case one plus one is more than two. I frequently stop the game during tactical 11 v 11 training sessions. Coaching players in the situation, that's what it's about. I'm aware of the fact that it sometimes drives players insane, but that's the best way to learn.

If we play eleven versus eleven, then I'm on the pitch with several other coaches. Each one of them has his own coaching approach. Michel Vonk pays attention to the central defenders for instance. Shota Arveladze coaches the striker and Patrick Kluivert coaches the striker of the opposition. Martin Haar then again pays attention to the 'little train' on the other side consisting of Stijn Schaars and Maarten Martens. Jan Nederburgh coaches the goalkeeper in conjunction with the defence. I lead the training session, but it is a rare occurrence that I have to wait a bit for the continuation of the training, because the assistant coach is still busy with his situational coaching. At our training sessions it's about details. Therefore, for every position we need to know exactly what types of tasks and

functions we talk about. The players and staff need to speak the same football language."

We spoke to Louis van Gaal during the international break, prior to the game versus Ajax (2-0). That week he's missing as many as 11 players due to obligations with their respective countries. Training 11 v 11 then isn't opportune, but for Van Gaal this doesn't mean we could call this a lost week of training. You're also able to train match orientated situations in smaller numbers. This time the objective of the training is to disturb Ajax's type of game in an early stage. This contrasts, because the 'usual' style of play from AZ was to drop off a bit when the opposition had possession.

Louis van Gaal: "You don't only train your own style of play during an 11 v 11 session. During the week of international matches Gill Swerts, Sébastien Pocognoli and Ari were present. We've been able to train the communication between the wing-back and the striker very well that week. First without resistance, and subsequently with resistance. The goal is to make Ari have better judgement at the right moment to request the ball and that he knows how he

can ask for it. He mainly has to move around the area of the front post. On the other hand, the wing-backs still need to improve their distribution of the ball to the striker at the right time and then behind the defender. Eventually the main purpose is Ari scoring. This is a drill I used many times last season as well, but now the chances are suddenly converted better. Ari's goal against Twente was one of those cases. Martens provided a cross behind the defenders of Twente and Ari scored.

Scoring is also a quality. I've always found Gerd Müller a moderate player, but he did manage to put them in the net! Whether someone remains cool when he arrives in a scoring position, I can simply see from the very first training session already. We have a new player in the second team who's not performing at his optimum yet in training sessions football wise, but he does score all the time. Players who have to work with me, often have to get used to playing football in small spaces."

'Players who have to work with me, often have to get used to playing football in small spaces.'

DEFENDING

Louis van Gaal: "The interpretation of the wing-back position depends on the formation we deploy, but generally speaking, the player in this position has to be able to cover a big space on the pitch. He has to be capable to build up and join the attacks at the right time. I expect a good striking technique for the cross. I deliberately start with all types of aspects that are important during the possession phase.

Every team can defend. If you reduce the spaces very well as a team and everybody

conforms to the tactical agreements when the opposition have possession, then defending is easier than attacking. I don't agree with the perception that we have a structural shortage in the training of

defenders. Then they are complaining about the lack of a right winger, and then it's a goalkeeper or a right back. These are all tendencies, which are usual in football. Brett Holman can function well in various positions. He came in for Martens, De Zeeuw and Van der Velden. He would also be capable of playing in El Hamdaoui's position."

THE HUMAN AND FOOTBALLER

Louis van Gaal: "My whole life I've believed in the 'total human' principle and I don't solely look at a footballer who's only having to play the ball from A to B. I also pay attention to the person in question, his behaviour and thus not only his qualities as a footballer. This principle has an impact on my assessment and approach of every human and thus also on every footballer. I'm curious about the motivation of each player to play in a certain position.

And I'm curious about the reaction of the player to my vision of him in relation to his teammates or the team. It's good to stay as close as possible to the identity of each player. In which position, what combination and with which players does he perform the best? For Mounir El Hamdaoui this has been quite successful this current season. It's no coincidence that he scores so much all of a sudden. He plays in a position which lies very close to him. It's always about what a player wants and how I as a coach can help him on his way.

On the other hand you can oppose this with the fact that David Mendes da Silva plays in several positions with us. He has occupied the position of right back, defensive midfielder, right midfielder and right forward. I basically 'use' him in the interests of the team or club. This is namely the interest that I, as a coach, have to pursue and it can be different from the individual interest. Being capable of playing in multiple positions, however, is also a quality of Mendes da Silva. He's multifunctional and specifies himself that he doesn't have much difficulty filling in other positions different to his preferred choice which would be as a defensive midfielder. I pick Stijn Schaars in that position, but because I want to select

Mendes da Silva as well, I have to shift him. The solution then often lies in the fact that he'll play in a different position. It's no coincidence that he managed to reach the Dutch national team once again. On the other hand, Schaars would have difficulty qualifying for the first eleven when Mendes da Silva plays as a defensive midfielder."

PERSPECTIVE

It's common knowledge that Louis van Gaal first invites potential AZ players for a conversation before a transfer gets completed. During this meeting with the player, the coach wants to know more than many of his colleagues.

Louis van Gaal: "The essence of top sport is that you're being measured against your teammates (first eleven/substitutes) and subsequently with the opposition (winning/losing). I have confidence in every player in our squad. Therefore, my decisions don't have anything to do with trust, but with the comparison between the players. The conversation I have before a transfer gets completed can also result in us parting ways. This could happen from both sides and is also influenced by other possible offers on the table for that player. Before we talk about football, I first want to know more about the private situation of the player; what is his education, does he have a relationship, kids? Afterwards I'm interested to know what the player thinks of his position at his current club. Then the time comes to discuss our expectations if he ended up playing for AZ. During this discussion we also use the board. I also want to know what the player in question expects from me as a coach, and the club.

During the first conversation with Gill Swerts I told him that in the first instance I

had a position for him as a right back in mind. We've also discussed in what other positions he could possibly play and what his perspective would be at AZ. This is important for a player to know. Despite handling this with care, I have players in the squad who have less perspective on playing time. Then they are in third place

for a certain position. Such a player will go through a hard time if there aren't many injuries. However, this doesn't mean that he doesn't stand a chance in his position. He's able to earn his spot, just like Martens, De Zeeuw and Van der Velden did in the course of this season."

"Schaars has a positive impact on the top sport climate."

"In our style of play Mounir el Hamdaoui has more freedom."

"We see him as a second striker."

Defending a Free kick: Each player is sharply focused on his own 'man'

THE MENTAL ASPECT

Louis van Gaal: "At AZ the players have to fill in a questionnaire each week. From their answers I can conclude where they stand. Often I already see this on the pitch during the week, except I don't have any knowledge of the cause then. By individually guiding the players on this area, we try to tap into the situation sooner if that's necessary. We can then deploy specialists very concretely, who can assist in solving potential problems. It's important we show an interest in the human being behind the footballer. We want to help him to deliver a performance, with the knowledge that this has to happen under resistance of the opposition, the decisions of the referee, the spectators, the media, but also from their immediate surroundings. In addition, there is progress to be made in the guidance of youth footballers in the Netherlands. The world is complex.

'Unfortunately there is still only little hands-on expertise on the mental aspect.'

It keeps getting harder to focus on one goal. This is caused by the zapping culture. Also at AZ we have special attention for the guidance of youth players regarding the mental aspect. It's of great importance that you're able to focus in top sport. Everything has to be targeted to achieving your goal, but on the other hand you'll still have to deal with lots of resistance in your career as a football player. Unfortunately there is still only little hands-on expertise in this area. Many sports psychologists don't have a background in the world of football (coaches). Someone who's specialised in, for instance, training the mental resilience has to be willing to work under the responsibility of the head coach. More preferably, he's a football coach with a speciality in the subject of mental resilience."

KIT MAN

Rejuvenating can be done with the players, technical staff, but also with other staff members. Similarly, Louis van Gaal has appointed a new kit man.

Louis van Gaal: "A good kit man has to work alongside the head coach. I shouldn't have to tell him what to do all the time. He always has to be there for the players or staff. This means you have to be present a considerable amount of time before the players arrive. After the players have departed, the kit man is at the club for at least another hour. It's an intensive task and you almost don't have a day off. It's also better to be single for this type of work. This maybe also goes for the position of a coach, but he does get compensated for it royally."

VIDEO ANALYSIS

Louis van Gaal: "An experienced coach, one that has gained knowledge throughout the years, builds his own vision. Actually I refined my vision on football thanks to the experience I've acquired. I deliberately named certain aspects as the four key moments in football, so I can make these things more clear to the players. And trainable! The way in which I prepare players for a match basically doesn't differ much from 30 years ago. However, we do have other tools at our disposal. The chalkboard has been replaced by DVD footage and PowerPoint presentations. At AZ we have Max Reckers working for us as a technical match analyst since last season. We've created the software ourselves, based on my vision as a coach. Reckers

originally comes from the hockey world, where they are much further in the development in technological areas for supporting the coach.

'An experienced manager, one that has gained knowledge throughout the years, builds his own vision.'

Accompanied by a cameraman, it's Reckers' job to collect information for the video analysis system, which has also been divided in the just mentioned key moments. With one push on the button it's possible to watch and compare footage directly after a match. The day after the match I look back at a montage of the match with the technical staff and afterwards with the players. We don't only record the matches, but also the training sessions. The day after I'm often together with the players to evaluate the training. I also show what can be improved and what is going well."

Attacking Corner: In-swinging Cross to the Front Post

Defending a Corner: Far Post Protected

THE IMPORTANCE OF YOUTH DEVELOPMENT FOR DUTCH FOOTBALL

How can the Netherlands continue to compete with the 'big' nations?

Louis van Gaal: "I'm convinced that a Dutch club is still capable of winning the Champions League. The proportions in terms of budgets compared with clubs abroad are still about the same as they were in the nineties when Ajax won the Champions League. However, it is important to deal creatively with the available budget. The Netherlands has to exploit the good opportunities in the infrastructure, starting with the training programmes. I am a strong advocate of the centralisation of the training centres in the Netherlands.

Right now there are too many clubs which pretend to prepare youth players for professional football, and it is not so in reality. Our pool of talents isn't that big, but the best players should be training and playing with the best. This is only possible if the existing youth programmes are combined. The intellect has to prevail here over emotions. An additional advantage is that the best youth coaches are also together. We have to keep investing energy in training. Our remarkable way of training and football leads to success, history has proven this.

Which other small country has achieved so much success?

The danger exists that if FIFA or UEFA don't take appropriate measures in the development structure, that 10 year old youth players will continue to be bought by wealthy clubs.

That is what's going on right now and it would mean the deathblow for, among others, Dutch football. I haven't let anyone investigate this legally yet, but a possible solution would be if every connected football association would demand that young players can't move to another country until a certain age. Until you're 20 for instance, you remain playing football in the country where you were brought up. In my opinion such a measure will be sooner accepted than the so called '6+5 rule', which isn't feasible due to the European regulation in the area of freedom of movement of workers."

"I also look at the person in question and his behaviour, so not only at his qualities as a football player."

CHAPTER SUMMARY AND LOUIS VAN GAAL QUOTES

FORMATIONS AND STYLE OF PLAY

- 'It's not that important whether you play with one, two or three strikers. It's about the execution of the tasks and functions of all the different positions on the pitch. From every possible formation you'll end up playing in each zone of the pitch anyway.'

- 'As a manager you have to purely look at the qualities of a team at that given moment. All that matters is that it fits the players and the implementation of those players on the pitch.'

- 'Altering your formation isn't the only thing you can do as a manager. It's also about the interpretation which various players can apply to that same position. In addition, it's also about the balance in the team.'

CREATIVITY

- Louis van Gaal always likes to have at least three 'creative' players in his team.
- Van Gaal plays attacking football, always wishing his teams to build up play from the back.

DEFENDING

- 'If you reduce the spaces very well as a team and everybody conforms to the tactical agreements when the opposition have possession, then defending is easier than attacking.'

WING BACKS

'The interpretation of the wing-back position depends on the formation we deploy, but generally speaking, the player in this position has to be able to cover a big space on the pitch. He has to be capable to build up and join the attacks at the right time. I expect a good striking technique for the cross. I deliberately start with all types of aspects that are important during the possession phase.'

TRAINING SESSIONS

- 'At our training sessions it's about details. Therefore, for every position we need to know exactly what types of tasks and functions we talk about. The players and staff need to speak the same football language.'

- 'We don't only record the matches, but also the training sessions. The day after I'm often together with the players to evaluate the training.'

ELEVEN VERSUS ELEVEN

- Louis van Gaal uses 11 v 11 training a lot, practicing the days before competitive matches with varied formations. He explains that these are the practices where he can explain a lot to the players.

- 'I frequently stop the game during tactical 11 v 11 training sessions. Coaching players in the situation, that's what it's about. I'm aware of the fact that it sometimes drives players insane, but that's the best way to learn.'

MAN MANAGEMENT AND MOTIVATION

- 'My whole life I've believed in the 'total human' principle and I don't solely look at a footballer who's only having to play the ball from A to B. I also pay attention to the person in question, his behaviour and thus not only his qualities as a footballer.'

- Understanding the position players are comfortable in is key to get the best out of them.

- Players at AZ all did a questionnaire every week so van Gaal could find out any problems. 'It's always about what a player wants and how I as a manager I can help him on his way.'

- Louis van Gaal stresses the importance of high levels of performance and focus at all times. 'The essence of top sport is that you're being measured against your teammates (first eleven/substitutes) and subsequently with the opposition (winning/losing)'

YOUTH DEVELOPMENT

- Van Gaal believes the training centres in the Netherlands should be centralised.

- He believes that young players should not be able to move country until aged 20. This is to prevent the richer European clubs from acquiring all of the talent from smaller nations.

CHAPTER

8

The Importance of Tactics and Psychology

Text: Paul Geerars and Henny Kormelink

The Importance of Tactics & Psychology

Louis Van Gaal Has a Good Feeling about AZ

In preparation for our conversation with Louis van Gaal it's worth noting that there has been much written about him, but the stories were often superficial and mostly concerned ancillary matters. He made an exception for for us, even during a busy period with many competitive European games. Usually Van Gaal gives us, at most, 45 minutes for an interview. However, for us he allocated twice as much time to go deep into the technical matters of football.

The result is an indepth interview where Louis van Gaal once again clarifies why he's considered one of the top specialists of the Dutch football coaches guild.

'We apply pressure with too much risk'

The last time Van Gaal extensively told his story in De Voetbaltrainer dates back to 2001. Together with Rinus Michels he was gracing the cover of our 100th anniversary edition. Since then a lot has changed. After employment at the KNVB, top clubs FC Barcelona and Ajax followed. The next step to AZ Alkmaar came as a surprise to many, although Van Gaal doesn't have a problem with that.

Louis van Gaal: "The feeling with AZ was and still is good. The speed of action impressed me; a delegation of AZ (Scheringa, Van Geel and Gerbrands) flew to Sitges within two days of our first telephone conversation. Before my appointment as head coach I talked to Co Adriaanse on the phone. I wanted to hear his opinion and advice regarding a possible move to AZ. We made an appointment to discuss this in detail at my home. That appointment eventually ended up lasting the whole evening, where we also enjoyed delicious sauerkraut and sausages. That evening we spoke about the structure, organisation, accommodation, rules, and the norms and values within AZ. After these conversations with Co, in addition to what I already knew about AZ or what I saw in the media, I had a good feeling about the club. AZ has a philosophy that suits me. The players just act normal, work hard, and present themselves well in the media."

ONE STEP AT THE TIME

Van Gaal already signed a contract in January 2005. This gave him plenty of time to further analyse the qualities of the team before he officially started as a head coach.

Louis van Gaal: "It's true that I observed ten important games of AZ last season, such as

Ajax, Feyenoord, PSV and the European matches. You have to interpret this as 'my preparation' for this season. This is a significant advantage. Once I stood in front of the squad at AZ, I let my assistants Martin Haar and Edward Metgod lead the first training sessions. Therefore I was able to mainly observe and analyse from the sideline. In the beginning I basically kept everything the same as when Co Adriaanse was in charge. At the start of the specific preparation, where we discussed the tactical matters of the team, I also came across things which Co dealt with differently than I would have handled them through my vision. But because the players generally had a lot of trust and felt comfortable with the working method of Co, I decided to not drastically change everything immediately.

'Processing changes in details step by step'

Subsequently we played the first games. The players noticed that I trained differently than Co, but were also clearly comfortable with my approach. Therefore, I could process changes in details step by step. For instance, from a four-man defence to a three-man defence with a fixed playmaker in front of them. So that became De Zeeuw, who we brought in very late. This change was actually born out of necessity, because we were dealing with many injuries, mainly in defence. Kromkamp went to Villarreal just when he was able to start playing again. The defender Steinsson also arrived later from Young Boys. Under the supervision of Co, AZ sometimes also played with Opdam who would push up to the midfield, while a type of player like De Zeeuw is already there when I'm in charge.

Furthermore, in an ideal situation I'm more of a protagonist of a sweeper pushing up. Not the same player every time, but alternating, depending on the situation. This is also much more difficult for the opposition to defend. On the other hand it's not possible to play all games on the desired level with three defenders and one additional player in the midfield. That would be naïve.

Other details which I modified, relate to the area where the forward and right winger should play. I want them to change positions less. Their qualities lie in taking on the opposition. Then I prefer that the players stay within their position and keep the pitch wide. Especially in Alkmaar where opponents often play defensive, then you have to keep the pitch wide. When changing positions, the distances could rapidly get too small, then you push up more often through the centre of the pitch and it's too crowded there. I told Steinsson that he shouldn't close down the space in front of the right winger Sektioui. He has to stay away, because Sektioui is capable of passing through his opponent. The same goes for Arveladze, he should also stay away. That's a matter of 'reading' the match.

I do however want the centre-forward to make himself available on the side of the ball, but on our right side, that's a preparation to get the ball to the right winger. Afterwards Arveladze has to stay away. He should move into that space though at the left where Perez is playing. You need to offer options to Perez, because he is less capable of eliminating an opponent. Perez does have the ability, however, to pick the smartest football solution and he also has the speed to handle the execution of it. If he has more options, then the opposition will have a much more difficult time. So this has

something to do with the specific qualities of individual players. I also haven't changed anything about the changes in position between Perez and Van Galen who, in reality, aren't real left wingers."

Picture: Van Gaal prepares AZ for a victory against Lovech to reach the knock-out phase.

BUYING PLAYERS

What was your role regarding the composition of the squad for this season?

Louis van Gaal: "Since January I've attended the meetings of Martin van Geel about scouting. So I did have an influence on the transfer policy, but I found the squad to be well balanced.

'Goals can be bought'

There was a 'reserve squad' in place and I added a few players to that team. You ask yourself the question how you want to play and that's the main criteria to buy players on.

With the transfer of Shota Arveladze AZ bought goals.

'The 'type of player' also plays a significant role for me. I have a certain philosophy and a player has to fit to that picture.'

Schaars, De Zeeuw and Steinsson have been bought for those specific positions. We bought Koevermans for 'the other style of play ' in case we don't succeed with combinations. He could serve as one of the first eleven in the future, but he still has to develop himself first. Actually, the investment in Koevermans already paid off by him scoring against Samara, which meant that we qualified for the second round of the UEFA Cup.

'I think you can apply pressure with three players against four defenders in the front'

I also look at the statistics of a football player. Goals can be bought in my opinion. Just take a look at Arveladze. It's no coincidence that he scores so much currently. If you look at his career stats then he's around 50%. That's a fact. A striker doesn't lose that scoring ability. Scoring is a quality which you either have or don't. In that regard, Koevermans also has a high average. In addition, the striker we were looking for also needed to be able to play with his back faced towards the goal, because that fits our style of play. Both of them are capable of doing that. Arveladze always gets described as an experienced player. But experience has nothing to do with age. I've known several players who were very mature at the age of 19 or 20, and this was also reflected in their mature way of playing football. On the other hand, there are also players of 34 who play very naively. The fact that Cocu is of great value

to PSV is mainly because of his personality. He's capable of binding the players, but I haven't experienced him as a leader myself. Arveladze and Van Galen are also binding players within the AZ squad, but they aren't leaders. Those are becoming increasingly difficult to find."

PRESSING

In a previous interview, you asked yourself whether it was still responsible to play 4-3-3 at international level with basic principles such as defending forward, continually attempting to play in the opposition's half, thus giving away space in your own half. One of the trademarks of AZ under Adriaanse was the pressing, isn't that conflicting?

Louis van Gaal: "Now you guys mention a very interesting topic. One of the aspects which I haven't changed yet is the way of pressing. Co Adriaanse did it in a different way compared to my preferred execution. The players are feeling comfortable with the way of Co however and that's why we still do it that way. Ultimately, it's about the players, not me, although I still think we will apply pressure in a different way in the future. I expect the players to realise that there are various roads that lead to Rome. In addition, the tactical choices are also dependent on the qualities of the squad. And the composition of the squad will most likely change at AZ as well in the coming few years. What's different in the way of applying pressure is that fourth extra player behind the three forwards who are pressing.

In order to perform this the right way, a team has to be well balanced. We're not at that stage yet, however, we did play that way this season. It worked out quite well most of the time. During the away game

against PSV we also started very well, but after losing De Zeeuw we continued by playing with four defenders and that's when we began experiencing problems. This meant one less player in the midfield; the distances became bigger and couldn't get covered any longer. For me this was confirmation that it's better to press forward instead of employing a 'wait-and-see' attitude. But, it of course does matter how you choose to press.

I think it's possible to defend a line with three players at the back. If that's possible in the back line, with a lot of risk of course, then it should also be feasible at the front. In order to do that, the players need self discipline and need to take the responsibility to apply pressure on the opposition with all three players. In general, forwards are intuitive and creative players have greater difficulty performing this than defenders do.

I think I should be able to teach them this. The trio has to function as a team; pressing at the right time, closing down and release your man. This can be done on all levels, also internationally. It's about the guts of the team and the coach to close down the opposition immediately. But the qualities of certain players are so high that some players require backing up. By maintaining a consistent application of pressure, Ajax and Barcelona achieved great successes under my reign.

So the evidence has already been provided. We're in the middle of a process now with AZ which also hinges on awareness and insight. Right now we press with four players, because Van Galen moves forward. That's why we have a player less in the midfield. According to my own vision that's too risky. Against most Dutch teams it's still possible, but against the true top teams

you'll encounter a problem. Against Ajax we've been depleted during the first half because of this. At Ajax, Lindenbergh became the free man in the midfield due to our way of applying pressure. Ajax managed to connect to that free man, while other teams have more difficulties with it. I think my players will find this out themselves. Internationally we can expect difficulties sooner."

THE DIAMOND MIDFIELD

Louis van Gaal: "If my team plays with two forwards instead of three, then I'm an advocate of a diamond in the midfield. You then have more lines, which troubles the opposition. The opposing team has to choose between three or four defenders. If you do choose to play with a 4-3-3 formation against a team that deploys a diamond in the midfield, then the full backs have to move forward to mark the midfield of the opposition, but it's not always possible to cover that distance. Then the deepest lying midfielder of the opposition is free. You can solve this by making your midfielders move forward to press the deepest lying midfielder, but there is still a trail of players behind them. That's the moment when you have to keep the transitioning going. For instance, Germany dealt with this very poorly in the first half against the Netherlands."

VIDEO ANALYSIS

Louis van Gaal: "At AZ, Edward Metgod makes use of hardware and software called Sportscode Elite, which has been used by all Australian sports teams at the Olympics. It suits us very well. We now receive more data about the players in the medical area, but we're also able to assemble footage in sequence for or about each player more easily. I find it an improvement on what I developed myself at Barcelona. That came down to the same thing, but I can request data easier right now. In addition, I'm also able to assemble footage in sequence much quicker for the match analysis."

FC BARCELONA

The way Barcelona are playing football must appeal to you as a football enthusiast…

Louis van Gaal: "Barcelona plays football in a way of which I think a top team should play. Pressing forward, playing football to entertain the audience. Picking the right moment to push up the sweeper goes less well, but with Puyol and Márquez in the centre this has been improved a bit. There is an excellent balance in players who can keep the ball, players who can win the ball and creative players who can just enjoy themselves up front. The midfield is outstanding. Xavi and Deco continually ensure that there is a connection with the creative players and the forwards. Right now that's a requirement in top football. This doesn't necessarily mean that FC Barcelona will definitely win the Champions League though, because defending is still always easier than attacking. The last couple of years we've been seeing a tendency with coaches that say the opposition can have the ball. The transitioning moments have become the most important in football. Teams with good defensive organisation benefit from this.

'Defending is still always easier than attacking'

Messi and Ronaldinho are two amazing players. They have a lot of football ability. Since Messi has the ability to eliminate an opponent, you shouldn't close down that space, but keep it big instead. Messi is mainly left-footed and is positioned on the right, while Ronaldinho is positioned on the left and he's mainly right footed. For instance, that's how I played with the

Netherlands against Andorra. You'll then get more in-swinging crosses. I find them the most dangerous, especially if you know that you'll be in the opposition's box often. If you get in front of the opposition's goal only occasionally, then it's perhaps better to use out-swinging crosses. With an in-swinging cross it's much more difficult for a goalkeeper to come out, because somebody could get in the way. Another advantage of a left footed player on the right is that the player can also go inside and then the ball is on his strongest foot. Robben has managed to and will continue to score like this many times.

In modern football the early cross has become more important than the necessity to reach the by-line. When an early cross is given, then there is still space between the defence and the goalkeeper. You then have more speed which makes it difficult to defend.

Within a 4-3-3 formation my preference is to have a midfield with 2 sitting players and a 'number 10'. The striker should always have support. At Barcelona I always played with two shadow strikers. For the opposition this was a surprise, but to play that way you should have those specific qualities at your disposal. Rijkaard also managed to find them in Deco and Xavi. Behind them Edmilson is positioned, who is the right guy to close down the space. Thus, this had to do with balance. He has players who can win the ball like Oleguer, Edmilson and Puyol; Deco as well, because he can do everything. And I think that the statistics prove that Xavi also falls under that category, because he's very intelligent. In the centre there is a block with Puyol, Marquez and Edmilson. Van Bronckhorst is a running man and Ronaldinho is in need of that, because you then offer him more options. And ultimately there of course is

an excellent forward, Eto'o. Look at that goal against Real Madrid for instance. That really wasn't that easy.

If you play with only one sitting midfielder, you have more defensive security. On the other hand you can also say that you will then have an extra player in front of the ball, but that depends on the way you use the players. In my third year at Barcelona I played with the one sitting midfielder. I had Luis Enrique and bought Jari Litmanen. The fact that Litmanen had to play five or ten metres outside the centre turned out to be very difficult for him. It's quite hard to find those types of players. The type of players that are capable to move forward, those that can hunt after losing the ball and those who are capable of providing that through ball.

What's important in each team is that all players have the same mission. In the beginning, Ronaldinho for example didn't have that. Now he does. Before his first goal against Real Madrid he was back in his own half. That says something about the Ronaldinho of 2005."

ATTACKING

You consider the organisation during ball possession as the most important principle for your game concept. Not many coaches do this anymore.

Louis van Gaal: "That's correct. But just go back in history. Are they still talking about the Juventus side that won the Champions League in 1996? No, but they do talk about Ajax of 1995, or of 1972 and 1973. Does

ARTIFICIAL TURF

The day after the interview, AZ takes on Middlesbrough in the Alkmaarderhout. Because of heavy rainfall the pitch doesn't look as smooth as usual by far. Of course the conditions are the same for both teams, but this really isn't in favour of AZ.

With artificial turf this would have been different. Van Gaal appears to be a strong protagonist of the use of artificial turf.

Decisive for the success of AZ: Louis van Gaal, Marcel Brandts (Director of Football) and President Dirk Scheringa.

attacking football appeal? Just look at how AZ gets approached. In general people say that the team plays attractive football. 'Football is a product and you have to sell it. But attacking is still always more difficult than defending.' These are amous words from Rinus Michels who used the defensive organisation as a basic principle as well, by the way, with a block of five or six players behind the ball. Rinus Michels, a beautiful man…"

'An important argument for artificial turf is Fair Play'

Louis van Gaal: "Many people in the world of football don't like the idea of artificial turf. In my opinion it is only a matter of time however. An important argument for artificial grass is Fair Play because then everybody plays football under the same conditions. This certainly isn't the case right

now. With Barcelona I experienced that they would make the pitch smaller by painting the original lines green just before our arrival, to give them an advantage as a side playing at home. You can call this the charm of the game, but it definitely feels different when you carry the responsibility of a coach.

When I was Director of Football at Ajax, I talked to Gertjan Verbeek and the players of Heracles about the artificial turf. In the beginning there were some doubts, but eventually Verbeek even decided to train on artificial grass in the stadium. The number of injuries was small. I think because the circumstances are the same every time."

THE 'MASTERPLAN'

During your employment at the KNVB you were an important figurehead of the Masterplan. Now a few years have passed by. How do you look back at the Masterplan?

Louis van Gaal: "The Masterplan wasn't only intended for the top, but also in particular horizontally. It's a comprehensive plan. It wasn't only about the pyramid structure, which is the best possible competition structure for youth players. Then the best play against the best and that's feasible in a country where the distances are small.

This however was only a small aspect within a much bigger plan. We're also talking about the integration of ethnic minorities in football, about football development, about the regional coaches that guide the coaches, about modules for coaches of the F-youth (U8). Because you make football more attractive horizontally, there is more of a chance that you will

develop better footballers at the top after a period of time. 'Queue training', whereby the youth players are standing in a long row before they can finally shoot on goal, we prefer not to see this anymore. As a result, the young players get more pleasure from playing football.

I was a figurehead for the Masterplan, but there are other people who have done a lot more work than me on it. When I say this, I think of people like Andries Jonker, Jan van Loon, Marc Esselink, Arno Pijpers, Marion Massop, Piet Hubers and Henk van der Wetering. They have meant much more to the Masterplan than me. The intention was also to give the U21 competition a different format, but I was barely gone at the KNVB and they reversed it. I think that the First Division should be open for second teams of regional training centres. In my opinion, the pilot of Twente/Heracles and Vitesse/AGOVV should be continued. They really deliver good youth academies. I'm thinking of Groningen, Leeuwarden, Alkmaar, Amsterdam, Utrecht, Enschede, Rotterdam, Den Haag, Eindhoven and Maastricht as spots for such regional training centres.

Then we still only have to make something up for Zeeland. In the current situation, the players who don't make it at Ajax, are going to a smaller club as well or not? I think we can save a lot of money by doing this and improve the quality of training centres, training the best and playing with the best."

JOSE MOURINHO

Louis van Gaal: "I had Mourinho as an assistant at Barcelona for three years. I found him to be very good at reading football. He analysed all the games for me. Under my supervision, the assistants also have to stand in front of the group, so he did this as well. Van der Lem did do this more often however and Mourinho would then assist me.

Furthermore, he also coached during a few friendlies and cup games. I did get a good view of him. His self-confidence and insight is tremendous and he was also ambitious. It was clear that he aspired to be a head coach himself. He succeeded in this. I expect the same of Danny Blind and Ronald Koeman for instance. Mourinho generally lets his teams play very conservatively. Of course his team attacks, but that's mainly because of the outstanding qualities of the players."

PSYCHOLOGY

Do you think mental coaching can be beneficial?

Louis van Gaal: "The most important thing for me within the team process is that they communicate with each other about what the objective of the team is and how you want to achieve that goal. Everybody has to know what his role is. That's the essence of team building.

If everybody joins that process, then the control is gradually taken over by the players. The coach then doesn't have to be 'the executioner'. That one player who perhaps is the discordant, is being corrected by the squad in an ideal situation. You can then hire a psychologist for this, but that person can never do it like the coach can. You can then better coach the manager. That's why I frequently talk with someone who's my coach in that area.

'As a head coach you're also part psychologist'

I wouldn't mind studying psychology later on, just to assess whether my judgment was right; looking for that confirmation. As a head coach you're also part psychologist. Experience helps during that process, but more importantly in my opinion is being human. How are you as a person and how do you relate to your surroundings? It's easier to do the things you like. They sometimes say that I'm a workaholic, but that's not the case. It's because I enjoy it. I'm a perfectionist or an achiever. Every now and then I do go relax on the sofa at home more often."

The Van Bommel issue: 'A coach can also make a decision based on a feeling or intuition.'

FLEXIBLE AND HONEST

The players sometimes say the following about Louis van Gaal: 'He's straightforward, clear, relaxed and social.' Is this true?

Louis van Gaal: "I'm not straightforward. Everybody thinks that, because that's the image I've got pinned down on me. I'm flexible. The fact that I still apply the pressing strategy of Co Adriaanse, while it doesn't match my vision is a good example of my flexibility. I do have persuasive power to pass on a different game philosophy to the team. But like I said before: it's not about me, but the team. We have applied that different type of pressing, but if I then see that it doesn't work, then I discuss this with the players.

It's then about what the players think, feel or what they are convinced of. Furthermore, I'm also clear, yes. Relaxed, yes, social? Yes, I think so as well, although others should say that about you. In addition, I must note that I think the characteristic 'honesty' is missing in that list. I'm very honest during the contact with my players. This definitely isn't always in my own interest, but for the benefit of the player. At the time I already told Ajax in October that I would be leaving. That wasn't in my interest, but in the interest of Ajax."

Ruud van Nistelrooy: Questionable for Van Gaal in a system with wingers.

NETHERLANDS

After your first term as Netherlands coach we've seen you frequently on television providing analysis about the games of the Dutch national team. How do you look at this Netherlands side, now as a club manager?

Louis van Gaal: "If you play like how the Netherlands team is playing, then I wouldn't position Kuyt as a striker on the right, but as a 'real' winger. It's then mainly about the type of player. Furthermore, in my opinion Van Nistelrooy can't play effectively enough with his back to goal. So you have to ask yourself whether you should select Ruud for the starting eleven if you're playing with wingers. But that's up to the coach. When the international games are approaching, Van Basten generally always calls. He asks me how I think certain players from AZ are performing. I assume

he's doing that with every player. The youth coaches of the KNVB call me up regardless of my status as a club manager. I also always receive feedback. I did that as well by the way when I was the Netherlands coach. Eventually the head coach of the national team makes the decision of course and not the club manager. And that's how it's supposed to be.

'Van Basten doesn't have to explain why Van Bommel isn't playing'

The whole country is now upset about the fact that Van Bommel isn't playing. It's the freedom of the coach to make such a decision. He will make the choices of what he thinks will lead to the best results. You don't have to agree with it, but it's the coach's call. We, the public, don't have to understand that decision. A coach can also make a decision based on a feeling or intuition.

He doesn't always have to explain this to me. The public should accept it. They are not the ones who carry the responsibility. Others from outside can easily judge without having any responsibility and without knowing all the details. But that's football because everyone has an opinion. Projections for the World Cup right now are quite useless. A team develops itself during the World Cup. Nobody gave England a chance and after the friendly against Argentina they are a favourite all of a sudden. As the head coach of a national team you'll only really be able to work with the squad once they've qualified for the final tournament. That's why I wished that I succeeded back then. Van Basten now depends on the club managers regarding the fitness of his players. Only during the tournament will it become clear who the

favourites are. And even then you still play against weaker opponents during the group stage.

It depends so much on whether the players are injured or not, what the coach does during the preparation period and the fatigue or 'hunger' of the players. And hungry, it's something the Dutch players are right now."

Flexible
Clear
Relaxed
Social
Honest

'During my time as Netherlands head coach my players weren't hungry enough'

WORLD CUP

Louis van Gaal: "I would love to experience another World Cup. I did have several offers on the table the past year for the position of head coach, but those teams failed to qualify. Those teams were Russia and Nigeria. Russia was interested before I signed with AZ, but eventually I opted for a club. I would have said 'yes' to Nigeria though. I think that the country does have some potential. Maybe because of my experiences with Finidi George and Nwankwo Kanu."

CHAPTER SUMMARY AND LOUIS VAN GAAL QUOTES

VAN GAAL'S PHILOSOPHY

- 'I'm honest during my contact with players. That's definitely not always in my own interest, but it is meant to allow a player to improve from it.'
- 'Queue training', whereby the youth players are standing in a long row before they can finally shoot on goal, we prefer not to see this anymore.'
- 'A manager can also make a decision based on a feeling or intuition.'

BUYING PLAYERS

- Louis van Gaal explains that every player he buys must fit into his philosophy.
- He believes that a defence must be worked on to become organised but that goals can be bought by purchasing creative players or clinical strikers. If their goal statistics were good before this is likely to carry on in your team.
- Experience is not important in terms of age, but solely the maturity shown on the pitch. 'Experience has nothing to do with age. I've known several players who were very mature at the age of 19 or 20, and this was also reflected in their mature way of playing football.'

FC BARCELONA

- 'Barcelona plays football in a way of which I think a top team should play. Pressing forward, playing football to entertain the audience. There is an excellent balance in players who can keep the ball, players who can win the ball and creative players who can just enjoy themselves up front.'

THE 'MASTERPLAN'

- Van Gaal believes a pyramid structure is the best way forward for youth development. Because the best play against the best, but if you make football more attractive horizontally, there is more of a chance that you will develop better footballers at the top after a period of time.
- Other important features of the 'Masterplan' include ethnic minorities in football, football development, regional coaches that guide the coaches, modules for coaches.

PSYCHOLOGY

- 'As a head coach you are also part psychologist.'

PRESSING

- Louis van Gaal always believes you can apply sufficient pressure high up the pitch with 3 attackers against 4 defenders. 'The trio (3 players) has to function as a team; pressing at the right time, closing down and release your man. This can be done on all levels.'

- It always better to press forward rather than have a 'wait-and-see' approach.

ATTACKING

- Louis van Gaal believes that the organisation during ball possession is the most important principle for his style of play and philosophy.

DEFENDING

- 'We expect our youth defenders not only to be able to defend, but they should also be capable of building up and providing a measured deep pass.'

WINGERS

- 'We should especially train multifunctional players, who are capable of taking over each other's position and are very aware of what their basic tasks are. On the other hand, the left and right wingers are very specific types of players. They don't lend themselves to be trained to become multifunctional players.'

- 'Wingers should be capable of successfully handling 1 v 1 situations, be very quick and have an excellent cross. I don't come across too many players with those qualities.'

- On in-swinging crosses... 'I find them the most dangerous, especially if you know that you'll be in the opposition's box often. If you get in front of the opposition's goal only occasionally, then it's perhaps better to use out-swinging crosses. With an in-swinging cross it's much more difficult for a goalkeeper to come out, because somebody could get in the way.'

INTRODUCING YOUNG PLAYERS TO TACTICS AND FORMATIONS

- 'I still believe that the 4-3-3 formation is the best system as a foundation for the youth academy.'

- 'From 16 to 23 you could focus on developing the tasks in different styles of play, including the 3-4-1-2.'

CHAPTER

9

Rinus Michels & Van Gaal on the Future of Dutch Football

Text: Henny Kormelink and Tsjeu Seeverens

The Future of Dutch Football

Louis van Gaal invariably calls Rinus Michels the 'Godfather' of Dutch football. Rinus Michels knows that Louis van Gaal is the coach that won the most trophies in Dutch football history. On the occasion of the 100th edition of De Voetbaltrainer both top coaches came together in their beloved Amsterdam to discuss the future of Dutch football. A unique documentation.

ANOTHER STYLE OF PLAY?

The elimination at the World Cup and the disappointing results of the Dutch top teams raise the question as to whether there still is any room at the top table of international football for the typical Dutch football philosophy with wingers, attacking, risky football and pressing in the opposition's half…

Rinus Michels: "It's clear that because of the current developments in today's game there have been essential changes, on and off the pitch, and at the top of professional, amateur and youth football. The job of a head coach at the top becomes more and more difficult because he has to keep adjusting the performance ability of his team to the increasing demands. In addition, the results have become sacred due to the vast commercial interests. Therefore, the pressure a coach has to deal with and endure has become bigger than ever. So you're obligated to keep your views as realistic as possible to grab the points. What type of style of play you use comes second in my opinion. Whether you like it or not, the result is what counts. That's what you are judged on at the end of the day. The style which involves most risk is a style where there is a lot of focus on

attack minded players. But what are the developments? The physical resistance is bigger than ever, so the art of defending has therefore become more demanding.

'The results have become sacred due to the vast commercial interests.'

Furthermore, the top clubs in many countries, including the Netherlands, have limitations in attracting the real top players. Only the true top teams in countries such as England, Spain, Italy and Germany are capable of doing this in the modern game. The other countries have to fish from another pond and this is at the expense of quality.

Those aspects alone don't necessarily have to prevent you from choosing a 4-3-3 formation, but they do influence the implementation of that concept. That's a significant difference. Take a look at Ajax for example. They can't afford to hold on to a 4-3-3 formation like they could a few years ago. That's because the current Ajax squad has too little quality in the key positions. Since the individual qualities are insufficient, due to the increasing resistance, the implementation becomes predictable, more so because in the traditional implementation the players are highly committed to certain positions.

If you subsequently don't have any success with that style of play, you start to make tactical alterations as a coach because you have to perform, something needs to happen. In my opinion you then have two options as a coach. You either review how the flexibility in the implementation of your concept can be increased or you'll have to opt for another concept unfortunately. It's possible that you don't have enough quality in your squad for that type of tactical flexibility. Then you'll have to think

of something that does lead to a higher productivity. Therefore, that second option is picking another concept, such as the 3-5-2 formation often used by Co Adriaanse. This choice certainly involves considerable risks. The development of a new style of play takes time, in fact, a lot of time. It's a very long process to reach a pleasant implementation. If you play with three defenders and five midfielders, then that's a whole other story positionally compared to 4-3-3.

Especially the transition from the build-up play and attack isn't easy. The players will make many mistakes in the beginning. The advantage of this system, however, is that it soon delivers advantages in defence. The types of players like Vierklau and Bergdølmo can now fully concentrate on their job as a man marker and therefore their shortcomings in building up are less visible. Chivu also feels more confident playing in the free role behind the man markers. This causes Ajax to concede fewer goals, get better results and then you comply with the primary objective which is winning!

But no matter what concept you pick, as a coach you can always cling to the principles which are typical for the Dutch football philosophy. Regardless of how important the result is, you can still strive to play positive football under any circumstances. That's not the same as attacking football, because that's not always possible! For me positive football is aiming to have the initiative, which automatically causes the opposition to back up a bit. This should be the starting point in a flexible implementation of any concept. For instance, it's possible to play very defensively with a 4-3-3 formation and in a very positive and attacking way with a 3-5-2 formation.

Where do you press, do you aim for the 1 on 1 in the back line?

Do you pick a pure winger on the flanks or a midfielder with attacking qualities?

Do you create a bit more operational space on one flank?

That's the flexibility in the implementation. I have difficulty with the predictability of the wingers' movements in the Dutch national team, but also at many clubs. Their task is to play outside the opposition's organisation through the flanks. But this becomes increasingly difficult due to the double man marking that often occurs and for a part also the lack of quality in these players for the highest level.

We don't have Beckham walking around in the Netherlands team or at top Dutch clubs. But his opportunism, speed and efficient crossing is an option which certainly is useful. You can't keep resorting to predictable attacking patterns. No, there has to be a lot of movement and positional changes. And once the cross arrives, the other forwards and for instance the attacking midfielder should also employ good positional movement in the box.

In Dutch football this is an important point of attention, because we're not too good at it. We often also don't think deeply enough about the build-up phase. We tend to choose to play the ball wide or pass the ball back sooner than providing that pass in behind the defensive line. Thinking and acting deeply requires the ability to anticipate. This more than ever has become a requirement and a quality to be developed in youth and professional football."

DUTCH FOOTBALL PHILOSOPHY

Louis van Gaal: "In my opinion there definitely still is a recognisable Dutch football philosophy. I base this for instance on the training model of the KNVB and the clubs. Almost all youth players have been trained in a 4-3-3 formation for the last 10 years. And most footballers still play that way once they join the veteran teams. At the top sometimes different choices get made, but underneath them the 4-3-3 formation is still often used as the foundation. That style of play is also the main thread in the youth academies of professional football organisations, the framework. So there definitely is a recognisable Dutch style of play. The champion of the Netherlands, PSV, play 4-5-1 during when the opposition have possession of the ball, but when they have the ball they switch to a typical 4-3-3 formation in my opinion.

I totally agree with Rinus Michels and that's why it will be difficult to just develop a whole other style of play so suddenly. It's a lengthy process to perfect such a new concept in respect to the defence, build-up and attack and prepare players for it. However, we have to ask ourselves the question whether a 4-3-3 formation with basic principles such as defending forward, continually attempting to play in the opposition's half and giving a lot of space away in your own half is still viable internationally.

'If it's apparent that the transitioning moment is becoming increasingly important in top football, shouldn't you adapt in that case?'

It's a risky style of play, which causes problems if one or two players fail. In a more defensive style of play like 3-5-2

you're less vulnerable if a few players aren't in good shape, because usually there are many more players behind the ball.

During my time at Ajax, and that's only a few years ago, I played with a 3-4-3 formation and most often there would only be four players and occasionally five players behind the ball. What you see now in international football is that the coaches don't mind if the opposition has the ball and they let their teams play the long ball, because they find the build-up too risky. No, you first handle your opposition on your own half. Subsequently you'll search for the highest productivity and this often gets found during the transition from defence to attack when you win the ball. First create that space for a deadly counter and then strike. In this way, Hector Cúper of Valencia managed to have great success and that approach is gaining more and more adherents.

That's a whole other philosophy than that of most Dutch coaches. We, Dutchmen, want to have as much ball possession as possible because we tend to think the chance will be bigger to dominate an opponent. But if it becomes apparent that the transition phase becomes increasingly important in top football, shouldn't you adapt in that case? You should at least think about it. And again, another choice has far reaching consequences for our training model. Why do we not develop the types of defenders that the Italians do? This has everything to do with our current view on how the game has to be played. We expect our youth defenders not only to be able to defend, but they should also be capable of building up and providing a measured deep pass. We find those buildup qualities just as important and that automatically generates a different type of defender at the end of the process. So if you decide to

pick another direction, then it will definitely have far reaching consequences in the long term."

Rinus Michels: "It's true that choosing a completely different style of play will have major consequences for your training model. One can question whether you should sacrifice your philosophy for the immediate interest that a coach of the first team has regarding the match result. Take a look at Real Madrid for instance. At the beginning of last season they had a phase with very poor results. The coach then made the same tactical decision as Co Adriaanse now did at Ajax! Vicente del Bosque also traded the 4-4-2 formation for the 3-5-2. All of a sudden more matches were won and the problem seemed solved. Then you see the phenomenon emerge with the public, who desire a bit more of a show from a winning team. Because the selfconfidence and form were back, the coach of Real Madrid ultimately opted for a 4-4-2 formation again.

As what I already said before, you can also apply some more defensive features in that concept. Again it's constantly about the necessary tactical flexibility of the coach and the team to make the circumstances their own. In 1988 we became European Champions without the use of specific wingers. After losing the opening match against Russia, I tried to find a better balance. A deep positioned Van Basten and behind him an offensive Ruud Gullit required compensation. So I took out the specific winger Van 't Schip, who could also deal with the resistance at that given moment, for Erwin Koeman. On the right Vanenburg played, also more like a midfielder. That tactical flexibility within a concept, that's what it's all about. That's a matter of an instinctive feeling, of having an eye for details. If that ability is

sufficiently developed in a coach, then he doesn't have to change a whole concept structurally."

Louis van Gaal: "For me tactical flexibility also entails that you should not hold so strictly to a 4-3-3 formation. I already said a couple years ago that we should especially train multifunctional players, who are capable of taking over each other's position and are very aware of what their basic tasks are. The defensive blocks have become so strong and so deep, that you're forced to work with positional changes.

On the other hand, the left and right wingers are very specific types of players. They don't lend themselves to be trained to become multifunctional players. Wingers should be capable of successfully handling 1 v 1 situations, be very quick and have an excellent cross. I don't come across too many players with those qualities. Just try to mention three right wingers of world class level. You would have to think about it for a very long time."

Rinus Michels: "Correct. Even Figo and Beckham do not fit the requirements which we want to set for wingers. They don't allow themselves to be limited to that one position, because then even moves from these two players with exceptional qualities become too predictable."

WINGERS

Louis van Gaal: "The resistance specific wingers have to deal with is becoming so high at the top, that we have to ask ourselves whether we should continue with a concept where such players have an essential role. After Overmars and Zenden there are still no immediate successors for their positions. In addition, during the past three years I've

experienced more and more players who either didn't want to or in any case reluctantly played on the flanks. They have the feeling that they are less involved in the game in that position.

Therefore, the affinity with the game isn't big enough in their opinion. You should take that into consideration as well. Rivaldo at Barcelona was such an example and Overmars for instance thought he could be of better value when positioned behind the strikers. The possibilities for a winger are quite limited. You can go towards the inside or through the flanks. But the options for the move through the flanks are being limited by the sideline, causing the resistance of the direct opponent to be optimal. And then I haven't even spoken about the double man marking. Then all that is left is the move through the inside. For example, that's why you see many left footed players on the right and many right footed players on the left in Italian football. But when making a move through the inside you'll quickly end up in a funnel with excellent defenders."

Rinus Michels: "Everything relates to resistance and the players' qualities. At Willem II, Hans Westerhof selects two specific wingers, Abdellaoui and Ceesay, and he gets a lot of recognition for it. On the level Willem II acts, they comply with all requirements. They can move well, are quick and can deliver good crosses. But at the highest level of football the resistance is much bigger and these two players would most likely come up short on meeting these demands. So everything isn't as easy as it seems."

Louis van Gaal: "When you notice that only a small number of top talents break through as a winger, that more and more

players are struggling with the role and the tasks they have to fulfil in that position, and that the opposition's resistance only increases, should you then hold on to a 4-3-3 formation? Should I continue to opt for this concept if I keep experiencing problems during the allocation of those positions or should we spend more attention to the specific training of wingers? For how long did the Dutch national team not have any serious problem on the right side? Just take a look at all who've played there: Ronald de Boer, Talan, Zenden, Overmars, Makaay, Hasselbaink and for example Bergkamp and Boussatta under my predecessor. It's not even a problem of today and age: EC '88 Vanenburg, WC '90 Kieft, EC '92 Gullit, WC '96 Ronald de Boer... You can hardly call them specific wingers."

'As a coach, during the past three years I've experienced more and more players who either didn't want to or in any case reluctantly played on the flanks'

Rinus Michels: "Dutch coaches tend to say: 'We will always rely on our own style of play.' That's admirable, but not always realistic. There are games where this isn't a smart thing to do, considering the force of the opposition and the qualities of your own. Louis van Gaal rightfully asks himself: Do you have to continue choosing for the 4-3-3 formation, if the implementation for those positions remains a problem on the flanks? In my opinion, therefore, the current question is whether the quality of the Netherlands team is sufficient now and in the near future to choose for tactical flexibility within that concept or should you definitely choose another style of play? That's a difficult matter."

BREAKING POINT

Louis van Gaal: "We're at a breaking point indeed. The supply of specific forwards for that kind of level is very small and you immediately get in trouble once Zenden or Overmars are injured or out of form. Furthermore, if it then turns out that the qualities of the Netherlands team stand out much better with a different style of play, should you then still hold on to (variations) of a 4-3-3 formation or do you choose another direction? A different approach, for instance, we have six centre forwards at international level: Kluivert, Van Nistelrooy, Hasselbaink, Van Hooijdonk, Vennegoor of Hesselink and Makaay. If you choose the 4-3-3 formation, then many of them won't be selected to play each match."

I agree with Rinus Michels that subtle tactical changes within a concept are also an option, but then you have to realise that it's about at least 2 or 3 players, whose tasks should be geared towards each other. For instance, I don't believe that you can give a player like Figo the freedom to play in the midfield for a part of the match, while the flanks are not occupied at that given moment. It shouldn't be the case that two players end up in the same zone after changing positions. Then the balance is disrupted immediately. So the tactical flexibility is also very crucial. But of course I've tried this with the Dutch national team. I played against Turkey without a right winger. To speak in the words of Rinus, I made sure there was operational space on the right side, where Van Bommel had to appear well timed throughout the midfield. In the highly charged match against Spain I went for a 3-4-1-2 formation. We didn't play very Dutch-like if you look at the execution and that wasn't good for my football heart. But we did win with a 2-1 score and that with only a half fit squad.

'We will always rely on our own style of play.' That's admirable, but not always realistic.'

Rinus Michels: "So that turned out to be a good choice for that one match. But you can't immediately come to that conclusion that you will pick the other system from that moment on. You'll undoubtedly experience complications in the execution during the next games. You won't succeed to teach a team all details of a new system on a nod and a wink. You'll need a longer time for it. For instance, a preparatory period before a World Cup or European Championship, when you have the squad at your disposal for many weeks. Maybe you can also use friendly games and the period before the next qualifying game. But then you should accept that it will be a process of trial and error. Will you get the time for this?"

IMPLEMENTATION

Louis van Gaal: "Now indeed the time has come where you could introduce a different style of play. I've used several players in the past year, because I gave many young talents a chance. And if I analyse the qualities of those players, I have the feeling that they can play in a 3-4-1-2 formation. But a feeling, even though it's based on a thorough analysis, isn't a guarantee.

We should first develop this new concept and then the games will tell whether we can also carry out that style of play under the highest resistance. And the story of that tactical flexibility of course applies to 3-4-1-2 formation as well. One time you choose a player with more depth on the flank, such as Overmars, Zenden, Bouma or Petta on the left and the other time you can maybe choose more of a corrective type of player, like Bogarde. On the right, players like Oude Kamphuis and Ricksen could also possibly be an option, because they play in that position at their clubs, but you can also think of Landzaat, who in turn has other qualities. In the attacking line you can select three of the six forwards.

Kluivert has proven that he possesses exceptional qualities for the position of a number 10, but Bruggink, Seedorf or Overmars could play there as well. Then you still have five players for the two central positions up front. I don't see any problems in the back either. Cocu or De Boer having the free role and as man markers for instance, on the right Reiziger, Stam or Melchiot and on the left Hofland, Bogarde or Numan. But there are also more possible options in that line.

In the centre on the midfield you have players like Van Bommel, Davids, Cocu,

Bosvelt, Van Bronckhorst and in the longterm maybe a player like Van der Vaart at your disposal. It's not about the names and there will undoubtedly be other players in the future who qualify for that position. I just wanted to note that we have sufficient players with specific qualities, who could function within a 3-4-1-2 formation. And again, you never know at which pace certain players will develop themselves, but I intuitively think that the real big talents could also operate within that system.

Ajax already plays like that in the Netherlands and many teams will be out for the count, because they are not used to it. In Spain maybe half of the teams play that way and in Germany three quarters."

Rinus Michels: "Of course, for Dutch standards it originally is a quite defensive style of play with a decent number of players behind the ball. The question is

whether it suits our culture. But obviously you can also play attacking football with a 3-4-1-2 formation, although the defensive features will stand out sooner. There is nothing wrong with that, but will it be accepted in the Netherlands? Is it possible to play with a different concept with the Dutch national team compared to most clubs in the Netherlands? Or do the managers of the Dutch clubs also have to choose another direction? These are the significant questions at this moment."

'Is it possible to play with a different concept with the Dutch national team compared to most clubs in the Netherlands?'

Louis van Gaal: "You'll first have to try it out. Put all things in order. How are you going to play for instance when the opposing team deploys three strikers? In that case I'm an advocate to play 1 v 1 at the back, thus applying a line defence. But the players on the flank should then make the spaces very small, so the three defenders will experience fewer difficulties.

We also have to figure out who will show up on the flanks in the operational spaces when we have possession. All these types of issues have to be put in order beforehand. If we really want to opt for this system in the future, then it's very likely that it could have consequences for the youth academy. I still believe that the 4-3-3 formation is the best system as a foundation for the youth academy. You could then play this way until the B-youth (U16) teams for instance. From 16 to 23 you could focus on developing the tasks in different styles of play, including the 3-4-1-2. I'm not saying you should use this concept in the future with the Dutch national team under any circumstances. However, based on the increasing resistance and the qualities of the squad, I think it's certainly a serious option for many games."

THE TRANSITION PHASE

At many foreign clubs you see an increased focus in the importance of the transition from defence to attack. Do we give this enough attention in the Netherlands?

Rinus Michels: "Other demands are imposed on today's top players. It's mainly about handling speed, accuracy and efficiency. This clearly has an effect on the training programme, because you have to develop these features in youth players in a way that will enable them to deal with the increasing resistance later on. 'Handling efficiency' means that you have to react in a fraction of a second, with and without the ball, defensively, in the build-up as and on the attack. You have to know exactly which option is the most efficient for the team in that particular situation in the match. That's different than the most efficient solution for you as a player!"

Louis van Gaal: "At the KNVB we then talk about the gain of the choice a player makes. And that's what we split again in terms like handling speed, overview speed and functional technique. But basically we mean the same as the description of Rinus. In the Netherlands we've been focusing on these features for years, because we try to reserve a lot of time during training for positional play in big and small spaces. That suits our philosophy in relation to us wanting to be the dominant team during the match. On the other side, we have coaches that opt for a counter strategy and don't want to be dominant at all, and spend more focus on the effectiveness in the transition phase. At such a moment it's possible that you have to deal with either an opposition that isn't well organised for a second or with an opposing team that even appears to be playing well organised under those circumstances. The latter was the case in, for instance, the games against Estonia and Andorra. Such teams just kick the ball away or lose the ball somewhere in the midfield, but the organisation is still standing together.

In such games you can hardly get any gains from the transition phase. But if you play against an opponent which attempts to combat you in a more open way, like Galatasaray did recently against PSV, then you can benefit a lot from the transitioning phases. In such games you keep seeing it more and more that the goals are scored thanks to an effective positive transition. Therefore, it's important to continue focusing on that specific moment and that's what we're working on very thoroughly now at the KNVB.

Rinus Michels and Bert van Lingen once split the game in three key moments: When the opposition have possession, when you have possession and the transition phases.

To devote more attention to that important transition, the term transition is split into the transition from attack to defence and the transition from defence to attack. And right now we're fully engaged into discussing how to make this trainable. This isn't easy. You'll have to develop drills which ensure that the players keep getting confronted with a constant turnover of possession (a transition moment). If you force them into that type of situation 100 times for instance, then they will recognise the space where they should dive to try and win the ball, mainly taking into account the position of the ball, the opponent and their teammates.

'Rinus Michels and Bert van Lingen once split the game in three key moments: When the opposition have possession, when you have possession and the transition phases'

And because you want to train as match specific as possible, you'll have to offer that learning moment in increasing spaces and that makes it even more complex. There is more insight required.

Rinus Michels: "That assistance results in getting more value from the transition phase and will ensure that the youth academy will be even further perfected in the Netherlands. It's necessary, because we don't have another strategy. The top teams are not rich enough to compete with, for instance, the top teams from England and Spain who qualify for the final stages of the Champions League most of the time. It's unrealistic to expect this from Dutch clubs. To maintain some sort of reconciliation, you'll have to invest more energy in the youth academies. Of course this then increases the chance that your best talents will be bought. You can't stop this. But if you increase the level of your training, you also ensure a high average with the rest. And there is definitely some room there. Several aspects can still be perfected. The 'Masterplan' will definitely play a role thereafter."

DIRECTOR OF FOOTBALL

After getting eliminated by Ireland a hot discussion started in the media about whether the coach of the national team should be allowed to spend time to working on the foundation levels. Or in other words, can the position of Director of Football and head coach of the national team be combined?

Rinus Michels: "I can speak from experience. I was Director of Football from 1985 to 1992. And although that wasn't the intention, I had to combine this position with that of Netherlands coach. During that time the training model still had to be laid down. The youth academy was given a complete new look in our country. So the programme still had to be formed. This has cost a lot of time and energy and during that phase it would have been very hard to combine this with the position of Netherlands coach. But the 'foundation' has now already been standing for a while and it's more about adjustments and expansion at the moment. That's something very different. I think the coach of the national team does definitely have an exemplary role in that area. The general guidelines about, for instance, how you could train players in the best way should always come from the technical staff of the KNVB in my opinion.

The implementation happens at the clubs and they do that in their own way. A head coach of a national team should at least be wise enough to form a good staff. I myself benefited a lot from the contribution of my employees."

Louis van Gaal: "I'm very clear about that. There is so much work left to do, that there actually should be a Director of Football next to a head coach of the national team.

At this moment, the KNVB (still) can't afford this financially. But I'm a hard working human being and therefore I won't avoid that challenge. That's how I worked at Ajax and Barcelona as well, by first structuring the youth academy and subsequently appointing a director of the academies and head of scouting. The KNVB will eventually also opt for that approach, but right now the money isn't available for it. Or other priorities are being set, such as the 'Masterplan'. Never before has the KNVB allocated so much money to improve all levels of the youth academy. So in the long term you can expect more gains, just like what happened in France.

Rinus Michels is right when he says that you'll mainly have to compose a good staff, especially for the implementation of a mega project like the 'Masterplan'. And that's what we've been very busy with and I more and more get the role as a guardian of the central thread.

Andries Jonker and Remy Reynierse are mainly involved in the implementation. There will be a new employee for the football development now Jan van Loon has departed to Willem II, and at the KNVB Academy we actually want to fill the vacancy which has emerged since the departure of Bert van Lingen. So I'm definitely not alone to do the job. But yes, if the results are disappointing, the media will always try to guess the cause. If we did qualify for the World Cup, then nobody would have had any trouble with me not restricting my work to that of the Netherlands coach solely."

REGIONAL COACHES

The pivotal role in the implementation of the 'Masterplan' is reserved for the new regional coaches, who also have to support the amateur clubs. Critics tend to argue that among them there are too many 'school teachers' and too few ex-footballers.

Louis van Gaal: "Just look at the requirements of a regional coach. He has to train people, ensure that boys and girls show up and especially continue playing football. In addition, they also have to pick out the talents and guide them. Therefore, a regional coach is a jack-ofall- trades, who needs to possess many qualities. Much more than just a football background, regardless of how important that is. I know many excellent professional footballers, who would be completely unsuitable for that type of work. You can't do that to them. If you have the required skills as a professional football player and you actually want to work on the basics, then that's an advantage of course. Either way the door is open for them. But how many former footballers have that ambition and those qualities?

It's impossible to completely carry out the 'Masterplan' with ex-footballers. Yes, you score easy points when you say that in the Netherlands, but in reality it's not feasible."

Rinus Michels: "That never ending debate is not pure. You keep hearing the cry that Dutch football is dominated by guys from the CIOS who were never active on a professional level. That sloganeering is of no use to me. You have to distinguish between the level at which the coaches are active. And from there on you have to determine which practical know how is necessary. Is it necessary for a person in a certain position to have participated in a European Championship or World Cup, that you've been a professional footballer, or is your experience as a player in (the top of) amateur football also sufficient to fulfil that task? If you have to coach on a lower level, then it shouldn't be a problem at all if you also gained a practical know how at a lower level.

You're in need of that practical know how to be able to read a match very well. But subsequently you definitely are in need of theoretical knowledge to distinguish the elements which then are decisive for the performance level of the team. Then comes the next important step, which I like comparing to a chef. Why is one chef capable of cooking better than the other chef with the exact same ingredients? This has something to do with individual talent. Subsequently the coach should also be able to transmit his vision to the group.

Just take a look at the coaches with a CIOS or academy background, like Foppe de Haan, Hans Westerhof and Sef Vergoossen. Their practical knowledge is less compared to that of coaches with a history as a top football player. However, this can still be sufficient for the sub-top. And in all other areas they perform more than enough in relation to the set criteria. In addition, they look credible based on their personality and expert knowledge. Then what's the problem? It becomes another story when they have to work with the absolute best in the world. Then your own status as a professional footballer can be a very important factor to get accepted by the players of such a team, to appear credible, also when things are going less well for a short time.

So basically you have to look at the level at which the coaches are active. That's decisive for the requirements you set for

them. This also applies to the 50 regional coaches. Obviously they need to have practical knowledge, but other core qualities can be equally important in that position."

ELIMINATION

In conclusion, who can be blamed for us not being present at the next World Cup and what are the consequences for Dutch football?

Rinus Michels: "Luckily I don't have to answer that question, because the expert is in this circle…"

Louis van Gaal: "Immediately after the game I said that both the squad and coach are guilty. We all made mistakes. It's not an excuse, but it is a fact that we had many injuries during the qualifiers the year after the European Championships. In the decisive match against Ireland, the players on the field I think panicked. Not one player stood up and took charge to be my extension on the pitch that way. We needed one that would tell team players to play in their own position again."

Rinus Michels: "That type of player is very important for a coach. I'm well aware that I've been very lucky, because I had a guy like Johan Cruijff for instance on the pitch."

Louis van Gaal: "After the match somebody asked me whether there was enough will in some players to defeat Ireland. Of course that will was present, because everybody realised what was at stake. But I already told my players during my time at Ajax that the will to win isn't sufficient. It's about the willpower, wanting to win that game by any means necessary. Under pressure of the extreme match situation, still being

capable to make the right choices, in the interest on an individual level as well as the team level. That's what I call mental hardness. Moreover, I don't completely agree with all the critics who raise major questions about the future of the Netherlands team and Dutch football. The supply of talents and successes always has its ups and downs. In two years it could look completely different again. People forget that the generation of 1986 with Gullit, Rijkaard and Van Basten were also guilty of being eliminated for the World Cup in Mexico.

Back then you could also read about the doom scenario in all newspapers. We would fall to the level of countries like Denmark, which was struggling at that time because all Danish talents moved abroad. And what happened? Two years later Rinus became European Champion with the Netherlands in Germany of all places. Who knows, maybe the current generation will grow rapidly and maybe a couple of veterans from this Netherlands team together with players like Van Bommel, Hofland and Van der Vaart, and who knows who else, will compete for the trophy in two years during the European Championships in Portugal. This depends on so many factors. In any case I won't participate on all that doom scenario thinking."

Rinus Michels: "I think that would be very wise. Is this the end of the interview?"

LOUIS VAN GAAL QUOTES

- 'Why do we not develop the types of defenders that the Italians do?

  This has everything to do with our current view on how the game has to be played. We expect our youth defenders not only to be able to defend, but they should also be capable of building up and providing a measured deep pass.

  We find those build-up qualities just as important and that automatically generates a different type of defender at the end of the process.'

- 'Rinus Michels and Bert van Lingen once split the game in three key moments: when the opposition have possession, when you have possession and the transition phases.'

- 'You'll have to develop drills which ensure that the players keep getting confronted with a constant turnover of possession (a transition moment).'

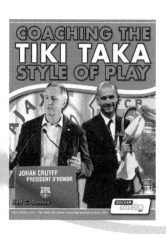

CPSIA information can be obtained
at www.ICGtesting.com
Printed in the USA
LVHW072037310120
645510LV00001B/1